COOKING LIKE A MASTER CHEF

{ **100 Recipes to Make the Everyday Extraordinary** }

GRAHAM ELLIOT

with **Mary Goodbody**

Foreword by GORDON RAMSAY

Photographs by ANTHONY TAHLIER

ATRIA BOOKS

New York London Toronto Sydney New Delhi

ATRIA BOOKS

An Imprint of Simon & Schuster, Inc.
1230 Avenue of the Americas
New York, NY 10020

Copyright © 2015 by Team Alliot
Photographs © Anthony Tahlier

First Atria Books hardcover edition October 2015

ATRIA BOOKS and colophon are trademarks of Simon & Schuster, Inc.

For information about special discounts for bulk purchases, please contact Simon & Schuster Special Sales at 1-866-506-1949 or business@simonandschuster.com.

The Simon & Schuster Speakers Bureau can bring authors to your live event. For more information or to book an event, contact the Simon & Schuster Speakers Bureau at 1-866-248-3049 or visit our website at www.simonspeakers.com.

Designed by Jason Snyder

Manufactured in the United States of America

10 9 8 7 6 5 4 3 2 1

Library of Congress Cataloging-in-Publication Data
Elliot, Graham.
 Cooking like a master chef : 100 recipes to make the everyday extraordinary / Graham Elliot with Mary Goodbody.—First Atria books hardcover edition.
   pages cm
 1. Cooking. I. Goodbody, Mary. II. Title.
TX714.E436 2015
641.5—dc23
                                                                    2015013063

ISBN 978-1-4767-9651-2
ISBN 978-1-4767-9653-6 (ebook)

To Allie, Mylo, Conrad, and Jedediah—the special seasoning that makes my life so darn tasty. You're the reason I do what I do and am who I am; without you guys I'm nada. XOXO

Contents

Foreword

I'VE KNOWN GRAHAM for more than two decades—we met when he was a young chef starting out in the business. For the past six years we've worked together as judges on *MasterChef*, which has been an absolute pleasure thanks to his fun, engaging personality.

Graham is one of America's most talented chefs, who cooks from the heart, and by making comfort food accessible his book will encourage budding home cooks to get into the kitchen and hone their cooking skills. The book has a wide range of delicious recipes to tempt every palate and give them the confidence to test out new techniques.

From healthy suppers for singles to cozy breakfasts for couples or full-on family feasts, it's easy to see why this book has so much appeal. It confirms why Graham became one of America's youngest four-star chefs.

Now there's no excuse. Get cooking.

Gordon Ramsay

Introduction

Cooking Like a Master Chef is a collection of recipes that I especially like. Nothing fancier or more complex than that. These are kitchen-tested dishes that represent much of what I value most about cooking. Before you get started, please read my "manifesto"—a highbrow way of saying I have three core beliefs to share. I first wrote this document when I was twenty-six and it's held up ever since. This helps me identify my early named primary tenets. I know it helps me get through the night—maybe it will help you, too.

MY CULINARY MANIFESTO

First, I believe in letting food taste like itself and so, not surprisingly, I am pretty intense about eating fruits, vegetables, and herbs when they are at their flavorful peaks. To me, these are nature's gifts to be cherished by everyone who enters a kitchen with the intention of preparing a meal. Because of this, I would rather eat food when it's in season and when it's grown close to where it's cooked, rather than rely on produce shipped in from some faraway place.

Don't get me wrong. I am not a fanatic. Most of all, I want everyone to cook. To push up their sleeves and get some good food goin' on, even if it means winging it now and then when it comes to the seasons. Throughout the book, I call out those recipes that are the most seasonal and make note of which veg and fruits are best bought from a farmers' market, but this is not a seasonal book. I simply want to put the seasons on your radar.

You may decide you only want to make squash soup in the fall, slow-cooked pot roast in the winter, and grilled chicken in the summer. Sure, that's how I cook, but it may not be how someone else does. My manifesto is this: be aware of the seasons, be aware of what's ripe and grown locally, be aware of the farmers who labor late into a summer evening to bring their crops to market.

Second, while there is no "right or wrong" when it comes to creativity in the kitchen, there are timeworn and time-honored methods and techniques that enable a home cook to come up with tasty meals. Some involve cooking seasonally, many others do not. All enable good cooking.

I learned the rules at cooking school and when I worked under some great chefs. Because I know what these rules are, I can break them—and I do. Before you decide to be as ornery as I am, understand that while I'm all about all cooks finding their voice and style in the kitchen, I honestly believe they must be their own harshest critic. I know I am.

For example, when I was the executive chef at Avenues, the high-end restaurant in Chicago's Peninsula Hotel, I decided to turn my deconstructed Caesar salad (page 54) into a soup. I thought: *What a great idea! We'll make a gazpacho-type soup with grated romaine and apples, garlic, and white anchovies and top it with a crispy Parmesan tuile.* Guess what? It was way cooler in my head than it was in reality, and in the end I deep-sixed the whole idea.

This is just one example of why I believe that beyond passion, a good cook must have respect for the ingredients and how they interact with each other—and the courage to know when they miss the mark. This is what creativity is all about: trying, succeeding, failing, and recognizing it *all*. And then tying on a clean apron and trying again.

Third, keep on truckin'. When cooking becomes a comfortable dance, we need to change the music to infuse our time in the kitchen with excitement and new energy. Are you with me?

I always tell the chefs who work for me that thinking outside the box is a significant part of the job. We're not manufacturing anything; we aren't building cars in the kitchen. Instead, being a great chef or talented home cook means being a spontaneous freethinker, not unlike a jazz musician.

Recipes are nothing more than ideas, and for each one there are any number of riffs that allow the resourceful cook to have fun. As you read through the recipes on these pages, I'll point out where you might want to change things up a little to make a dish your own, and when you should stick to the written word.

And it's always a good idea to cook the dish as I explain it at least once before you go out on a limb. Once you smell, see, touch, and taste it, you'll be better able to customize it to your liking.

So, how did I get from writing my manifesto to writing a book? It's been a long, strange trip!

I dropped out of high school to join a punk rock band, which is as good a place as any to begin my story. Like most punk rock bands, we didn't make a lot of money, so I found work in restaurant kitchens as a dishwasher and busboy. When I lifted my head from the stacks of dirty dishes long enough to wipe the soap from my arms, I realized there was a heck of a lot of creativity going on in this hot and steamy place. In some ways, it rivaled the creativity of the band. This was a pretty cool surprise for me, and when I realized I couldn't stop thinking about food, I decided to get an education. And that's how I ended up at Johnson & Wales, where I trained to be a chef.

MUSIC MAKES THE CHEF

I never stopped loving music. To this day, it pretty much sustains me, and whenever I can, I write, play, and record it. You can hear these tunes at Graham Elliot Bistro, my Chicago restaurant, and also find them on our website. These days I'm interested in acoustic-based music and put as much emotion into it as I put into my food.

Playing music is akin to cooking. For both, you have to understand the basics and then be willing to push boundaries. When you cook, the ingredients come together in the finished dish; when you make music, the various riffs come together in the final piece. Either way, getting there is half the fun, but you also have to keep your eye on the prize. As rock promoter Bill Graham once said of the Grateful Dead, "They're not the best at what they do, they're the only ones that do what they do." I think that pretty much sums up my approach to cooking: I don't claim to be the best, although I always strive for excellence. And I most definitely follow the beat of my own drum.

My love of music and its symbiotic relationship with cooking explains my relationship with Lollapalooza, one of the country's largest and most respected music festivals celebrated for three days every August in Chicago's Grant Park. I'm the culinary director of the festival and when bands I meet there play Chicago at other times of year, I invite them to the restaurant to share my food, my art, with them.

MOVIN' ON UP

Back to the story. After school, I was blessed. I learned from and worked with some of the best chefs in the country (Dean Fearing, Charlie Trotter, and Rick Tramonto, for instance), and enjoyed every day and every bite along the way. When I came to terms with the fact that I had eaten myself to 400 pounds, I figured it was time to take control. In the summer of 2013, I made a commitment to getting healthy. I worked out, ate more healthfully, and had a procedure called a vertical sleeve gastrectomy, which basically made my stomach smaller. I now weigh 250 pounds, which means I've lost 150 pounds and have more energy and am happier to be alive than ever before.

Along with these personal triumphs, my cooking style matured. What you'll find on these pages are recipes that make me happy and that celebrate both the foods I like to eat and the seasons that surrender them. (Despite my weight loss, I have not written a book filled with "diet" recipes! On the other hand, these aren't as over the top as they might have been if I'd written *Cooking Like a Master Chef* four or five years ago.)

I've worked at great restaurants and I've opened and closed a few of my own. Currently I'm pouring enormous energy into Graham Elliot Bistro on West Randolph Street in the heart of Chicago. When I'm not there, I travel around the country attending events and taking note of what America is eating and how our habits change—for better and for worse.

I also spend a lot of the year in Los Angeles shooting *MasterChef* and *MasterChef Junior*. Yeah, that's me. The fun guy on *MasterChef* and *MasterChef Junior*, alongside Gordon Ramsay. You know, the "nice one," the "Paula Abdul" of the judging panel. I'm the gentle giant with the bow ties, inked forearms, and white-rimmed glasses who every week comes up against Gordon's frenetic energy and plays to our more than six million viewers. Hey, Mom and Dad, I'm on TV!

TV AND ME

We've completed six seasons of *MasterChef* and three of *MasterChef Junior* on Fox, and I've been there since day one. It's been a wild, exhilarating ride, no doubt about it.

Here's how it went down: I'd met Gordon years before when I was twenty years old and had cooked with him at an event—one of my favorite culinary memories that I've cultivated over the years. Somebody from his camp reached out to let me know they were working on a new show to find America's best amateur home cooks. Would I want to be part of the fun?

I hopped a plane for California the next day, already pigeonholing the jaunt in the "what do I have to lose?" category. I'd cooked against Bobby Flay on *Iron Chef America* and had participated on two seasons of *Top Chef Masters*, so I was familiar with how TV worked. I guess it stood me in good stead; I wasn't particularly nervous and by the end of the day, one of the producers sat me down. "If you get this gig," he said, "it will change your life." "That's cool," I responded, not knowing the full impact the show would have on my life and career.

I red-eyed it back to Chicago and the very next day they called with an offer. I was back in Los Angeles a week later—my first lesson in how rare "long lead times" are in showbiz. When I walked on the set that first day, I was bowled over by its size, the number of cameras and lights, and the scores of helpful crew members making themselves busy. Whoa! Was this the big time or what?

As the show has developed, my role has developed as well. I'm driven by creativity and artistry, and love to hear the story behind the food as much as I appreciate the food itself. My approach when judging *MasterChef* reflects my cooking style. I believe American regional cooking is a looking glass into how we live and think about eating. Studying local dishes reveals much about a region of the country: how it's farmed, how it's fished, who settled it and when, as well as how it has changed over the generations. We're not so much a melting pot as a gumbo of regions and cooking styles. This may not be an astounding observation, but I think it's endlessly cool to explore.

After a few seasons of *MasterChef*, we came up with the idea for *MasterChef Junior*. I was in on the ground floor and have always loved the concept. As anyone who's watched the show knows, the kids are amazing. In fact, we had to go back to the drawing board when we started auditioning our first season's applicants. They were far more talented than we'd anticipated and so we had to kick everything up a notch or two.

Nowadays, I'm in California for three or four months out of the year shooting both *MasterChef* and *MasterChef Junior*. If you think the life of a television cooking judge is glamorous, it ain't. I get to the studio every day by eight a.m., and we work for ten or twelve hours with maybe twenty minutes for lunch. And this is six days a week. At the end of this period of time we have full seasons for both shows in the can and I can go home to Chicago.

When I was a kid, I spent a lot of time living by the ocean in Hawaii, so L.A. appeals to me and I truly love the little downtime I have. It's warm; there are beaches, palm trees, sunshine, and blue skies. And it's about as geographically close to Hawaii as the mainland gets. Plus, my family travels out west with me, so it's extra exciting for everyone.

SETTLING DOWN

My life growing up was different from the stories other chefs tell about theirs. I didn't have that grandma who stirred the pot of sauce all day, or the mom who called us into the kitchen to bake cookies for fun. I was a navy brat and between the ages of four and fourteen we'd moved from Hawaii to California to the Philippines and to Maryland and I'd attended ten different schools. I had the chance to spearfish octopus, hunt for monkeys in the jungle, and taste everything from dog to balut (Google it; gross). This turned out to be the most awesomely badass upbringing any Huckleberry Finn–lovin' kid could ask for, and it definitely influenced my cooking.

My kids won't have the same experiences, but my wife, Allie, and I believe in traveling with them as much as we can and exposing them to all sorts of foods and customs. My oldest boy, Mylo Ignatius (named for Ignatius J. Reilly, the protagonist in John Kennedy Toole's wonderful book *A Confederacy of Dunces*, which happens to be my very favorite work of fiction), is already a food critic. My next, Conrad Matthias (named after my mentor Matthias Merges, who helped guide me personally and professionally during my formative years at Charlie Trotter's), eats just about anything put in front of him at least once and is definitely the one most like me in the kitchen. He loves to cook, gets excited by weird ingredients, and never tires of exploring the restaurant. My littlest, Jedediah Lindsay (named after both my and Allie's dads), is still figuring out if he's as game as his brothers.

Without doubt, going to so many schools made me adaptable, both in the kitchen and on *MasterChef*. For example, as thrilled as I am to write *Cooking Like a Master Chef*, I don't personally follow recipes too religiously; instead I let the ingredients take me where they will. Allie, on the other hand, is loyal to recipes and does the majority of the cooking at home.

She has been the more focused and driven of the two of us from the beginning when our paths crossed years ago when we both worked at the Peninsula Hotel here in Chicago. These days, with the kids and their needs and me eating and living more heathfully than before, she is very into natural, seasonal, and organic food, which benefits the whole family. And we love to shop at farmers' markets whenever possible. Beyond the obvious freshness, we like the colors, textures, aromas, and variety of the fruits and vegetables, as well as the cheeses, eggs, and breads so often available, too.

My family will always be my number one priority, but walking the line between it and my professional life can be tough. All this comes down to wearing a lot of hats—TV host, chef/restaurateur, businessman, musician, and now cookbook author. And, most important, husband and father.

Leaf through these pages and find some recipes you want to try. Let me know how you like them, what worked for you and what didn't. We're on this journey together, and the highest compliment you can pay me is to try one, two, or more of the dishes I love.

COOKING LIKE
A MASTER CHEF

1
BITES and SNACKS

YOU KNOW HOW SOMETIMES you have a craving for something yummy but don't wanna pig out? Well, that's where these bad boys come in: small bites of pure goodness created to whet your appetite and sate any hunger.

But don't go crazy. As they say, too much of a good thing can end up being bad. While a hefty portion of a favorite might sound like a good idea, you could find yourself getting bored after a few bites. So, that's all you want—which makes the recipes here just about perfect.

Small in size but big on flavor, break these out when you're having friends over for a special dinner or wanna invite "the guys" over for the Super Bowl. Side note: These morsels of goodness are just as much fun to eat when you are hanging out by your lonesome. And a piece of advice: Prepare these beforehand if you can. That way you'll have more time to enjoy the party. Go Bears!

Smoked Marcona Almonds

{MAKES ABOUT 4 CUPS}

MARCONA ALMONDS ARE FAR more complex than the traditional variety we all grew up with. They are heavier, thicker, and crunchier and always come whole and heavily toasted (as opposed to sliced, blanched, etc.). The almonds pair perfectly with cheese and cured meats or, as in this case, are damn good simply on their own. (For more on marconas, see below.) We serve them as a free snack at the bar in our restaurant and people seem to enjoy them with a cold beer . . . hint hint.

PREP TIME: ABOUT 20 MINUTES, PLUS SOAKING
COOKING TIME: 20 TO 25 MINUTES

2 cups applewood chips	1 tablespoon salt
2 tablespoons sugar	4 cups marcona almonds

1. Put the applewood chips in a container and pour enough cold water over them to cover by a few inches. Let the chips soak while you prepare the almonds.

2. Fill a large saucepan with 6 cups of water and add the sugar and salt. Bring to a boil. Add the almonds and turn off the heat. Let the almonds soak in the hot water for 20 minutes.

3. Drain the almonds and transfer to a perforated pan for smoking.

4. Drain the wood chips and put them in a smoker, following the manufacturer's instructions. If you don't have a smoker, prepare a charcoal grill for smoking. Let the coals get hot and then sprinkle the drained chips over them.

5. Put the almonds in the smoker (or grill), cover, and smoke for a single cycle in the smoker or for 15 to 20 minutes in the grill. Let the almonds cool before serving.

The Marcona Almond Mystique
I gotta use the same words everyone else does when describing the fat, sassy Spanish almonds called marcona: sweet, tender, buttery, and delicate. "Regular" almonds—those grown primarily in California—are a little flatter, a little longer, and not quite as moist and flavorful because of their lower oil content. These days, marcona almonds turn up *everywhere*, which makes sense since they are damn good. Sure, you can use other almonds in any of my recipes that call for marconas, but try to find the big, plump M's.

Curried Corn Nuts {SERVES 4 TO 6}

WHEN YOU GRAB A HANDFUL of these corn nuts, you'll want to grab a beer to wash 'em down. We serve these at the restaurant, but they're super for the home cook, too. The curry is a little salty and tastes pleasingly of cumin. Everyone will love these.

PREP TIME: **ABOUT 15 MINUTES**
COOKING TIME: **ABOUT 12 MINUTES**

1 tablespoon olive oil

8 ounces packaged corn nuts

1½ teaspoons curry powder

1 teaspoon sea salt

½ bunch cilantro (about 1 ounce)

1. In a sauté pan, heat the oil over medium heat and when hot, gently sauté the corn nuts for 1 to 2 minutes.

2. Sprinkle the curry powder and salt over the corn nuts and cook, stirring occasionally, for about 10 minutes, or until crisp and fragrant.

3. Set the corn nuts aside to cool.

4. Chop the cilantro and toss with the corn nuts just before serving.

Root Vegetable Pickles {SERVES 4 TO 6}

I WAS INSPIRED BY ESCABECHE when I came up with this spicy mix of pickled veggies. Escabeche, a traditional Spanish-Latino dish of pickled fish, is served cold. I decided to try it with turnips, celery root, and parsnips, all classic root-cellar fare associated with cold weather.

PREP TIME: **ABOUT 10 MINUTES, PLUS COOLING AND MARINATING**
COOKING TIME: **5 TO 7 MINUTES**

½ cup pickling spices (see Note)

4 cups apple cider vinegar

2 cups sugar

3 baby turnips, cut into ½-inch dice

3 red radishes, cut into ¼-inch-thick slices

2 carrots, peeled and cut into ¼-inch-thick slices

2 parsnips, peeled and cut into ¼-inch-thick slices

1 celery root (also called celeriac), cut into ½-inch dice

1. In a large saucepan, toast the pickling spices over medium heat, stirring them with a wooden spoon, for 2 to 3 minutes, or until fragrant.

2. Add the vinegar, sugar, and 1 cup of water and bring to a simmer over medium heat, stirring occasionally until the sugar dissolves. Raise the heat to high and bring the mixture to a boil. Immediately remove from the heat.

3. In a large bowl, toss together the turnips, radishes, carrots, parsnips, and celery root. Pour the hot pickling liquid over the vegetables. Stir a few times to mix and set aside to cool. When lukewarm, cover the bowl and refrigerate the vegetables for 2 days. To serve, drain the vegetables from the liquid.

NOTE: Pickling spices are sold already mixed in the spice aisle of supermarkets. Most include cloves, mustard seeds, coriander seeds, dill seeds, allspice, peppercorns, and crumbled bay leaves. Some also include cinnamon.

Curried Corn Nuts

Root Vegetable Pickles

Avocado Hummus

Avocado Hummus {MAKES ABOUT 4 CUPS}

HUMMUS IS ONE OF THOSE THINGS you enjoy primarily for the texture. Smooth, thick, fulfilling without being filling (if that makes sense). Here, I decided to freshen it up for the warmer months by using avocado. If you switch out the ingredients and add jalapeño, onion, cilantro, etc., you'll obviously end up with guacamole. This is just as tasty and shows you're open to new things.

PREP TIME: **ABOUT 10 MINUTES**

1 (15-ounce) can chickpeas, drained and rinsed

2 cloves garlic, coarsely chopped

1 jalapeño, seeded and chopped

¼ cup extra-virgin olive oil, plus more for drizzling

2 tablespoons tahini

3 medium ripe avocados, peeled and cut into large chunks

3 tablespoons fresh lime juice

½ teaspoon sumac

½ teaspoon Aleppo pepper, optional (see Note)

¼ teaspoon ground cumin

Salt

1 tablespoon chopped cilantro

1 tablespoon chopped flat-leaf parsley

¼ teaspoon red pepper flakes

Shaved radish, for garnish

Cilantro leaves, for garnish

Sesame seeds, for garnish

3 to 4 pita breads, cut into wedges

1. In the bowl of a food processor fitted with the metal blade, pulse the chickpeas, garlic, jalapeño, oil, and tahini until nearly smooth.

2. Add the avocados, lime juice, sumac, Aleppo pepper (if using), and cumin and process until the hummus is smooth.

3. Scrape the hummus into a bowl and season to taste with salt. Fold in the cilantro, parsley, and red pepper flakes.

4. Serve garnished with a drizzle of oil and sprinkled with shaved radish, cilantro leaves, and sesame seeds. Serve the pita wedges on the side.

NOTE: Named for the Turkish town of Aleppo where the chile grows, Aleppo pepper is sold ground or crushed and adds a mild, pleasing, almost fruity heat to dishes. It's used widely in Middle Eastern dishes.

Grilled Portobello Mushroom Satay with Peanut Sauce and Cilantro {SERVES 3 TO 4}

THIS ENTIRELY VEGAN DISH screams of Southeast Asia. The ingredients for the peanut sauce pretty much grow together. They just naturally go together, too. It's so cool when that happens, especially when you think they have grown and been eaten in tandem for thousands of years. I use meaty portobello mushrooms in place of chicken or beef, which may be more traditional for satay, and while you could serve the sauce with either one, I especially dig it with earthy mushrooms. For an even smoother, richer sauce, stir in some silken tofu.

PREP TIME: **ABOUT 25 MINUTES, PLUS SOAKING AND MARINATING**
COOKING TIME: **20 TO 25 MINUTES**

MUSHROOMS

4 medium portobello mushroom caps

½ cup soy sauce

2 tablespoons canola oil

2 tablespoons chopped garlic

1 tablespoon chopped fresh ginger

1 tablespoon sesame oil

1 teaspoon Sriracha

½ teaspoon red pepper flakes

PEANUT SAUCE

1 tablespoon canola oil

1 tablespoon minced garlic

1 tablespoon minced fresh ginger

2 cups coconut milk

2 tablespoons creamy peanut butter

1 teaspoon mirin

2 tablespoons fresh lime juice

1 teaspoon rice wine vinegar

1 teaspoon dark soy sauce

¼ teaspoon fish sauce (optional)

½ cup chopped roasted peanuts, for garnish

¼ cup chopped cilantro, for garnish

1. For the mushrooms, put six 6-inch bamboo skewers in a shallow dish filled with cold water and let them soak for at least 20 minutes.

2. Using a kitchen spoon, carefully scrape the gills from the underside of the mushroom caps. Slice each mushroom cap into 6 long strips for a total of 24 strips. (Don't worry too much about the math.) You want enough strips of meaty mushrooms to fill up the skewers, but if one skewer holds 4 strips and another has 5, it's cool. Or you can use more skewers with only 2 or 3 strips. Whatever works for you and your needs.

3. Drain the skewers and thread 4 mushroom strips onto each one.

4. In a large, shallow bowl, whisk the soy sauce, canola oil, garlic, ginger, sesame oil, Sriracha, red pepper flakes, and 1 cup of water. Put the skewered mushrooms in the marinade and set aside at room temperature to marinate for 3 hours. While the mushrooms marinate, turn the skewers several times to make sure the mushrooms are well coated with marinade.

5. Meanwhile, for the sauce, in a saucepan, heat the canola oil over medium heat. When hot, sauté the garlic and ginger for about 2 minutes, or until they soften. Add the coconut milk, peanut butter, and mirin and whisk until all the ingredients are well mixed.

6. Reduce the heat and simmer the sauce for 15 to 20 minutes, adjusting the heat up or down to maintain the simmer. When the sauce begins to thicken, remove it from the heat and stir in the lime juice, vinegar, soy sauce, and fish sauce (if using).

7. Strain the sauce through a fine-mesh sieve into a bowl and set aside to cool to room temperature.

8. Prepare a charcoal or gas grill so that the coals or heating elements are medium-hot.

9. Lift the skewers from the marinade and gently pat dry with paper towels. Lay the skewers on the grill and cook for 3 to 4 minutes on each side.

10. Arrange the skewered mushrooms on a plate, coat them with the peanut sauce, and sprinkle with the peanuts and cilantro.

A Gift from Southeast Asia

I think everyone recognizes satays, although some of you prob just call 'em kabobs or skewers (which is cool; I do, too, most of the time). They're one of my favorite Indonesian imports (my very favorite being my chef-partner, Merlin Verrier), made when small, usually wooden skewers are threaded with chunks of chicken, beef, lamb, goat, or pork, charred, and served with a dipping sauce, generally a peanutty one. You gotta love these charmers. The satay here is made with portobello mushrooms, which I pair with a smooth, coconutty peanut sauce. Which, by the way, would be awesome with chicken, beef, lamb, goat, pork . . .

Truffled Popcorn {SERVES 4}

POPCORN REMINDS ME OF THE CIRCUS, carnivals, and the movies—and of being a kid. I started putting it on the table at the restaurant instead of bread, and wow! Instant hit. It's less filling and sets the tone for the meal to come: "This is going to be fun!" I also get a kick out of pairing a food that costs about a nickel (popcorn) with one that can cost thousands of dollars a pound (truffles), and so this has become one of my signature dishes. At Chicago's Lollapalooza, we sell close to ten thousand bags of truffled popcorn in a single summer weekend. You can make this with melted truffle butter and save yourself a few bucks!

PREP TIME: 5 TO 7 MINUTES
COOKING TIME: 2 TO 3 MINUTES

½ cup popcorn kernels

Corn oil, for stovetop popping (optional)

1½ tablespoons unsalted butter, melted

1 tablespoon truffle oil

1 ounce Parmesan cheese, finely grated (I use a Microplane for grating), about ¼ cup

2 tablespoons chopped fresh chives

2 teaspoons salt

1 teaspoon freshly ground black pepper

1. Pop the corn kernels in a standard hot air popper or in a covered deep saucepan with a little corn oil.

2. Transfer the warm popcorn to a large bowl and add the butter and truffle oil. Toss well to coat the popcorn with the butter and oil.

3. Add the Parmesan, chives, salt, and pepper. Toss well.

4. Transfer the popcorn to a brown paper bag or serving bowl. Serve immediately.

To Truffle Ahhhh! Say "truffle" to a chef and chances are he or she will swoon. Seriously. We love 'em, but because they are so damn expensive, chefs rarely cook with them and most home cooks never experience how truly awesome they are. You might find white truffles shaved over pasta, or black truffles chopped fine and mixed in a terrine at high-end restaurants, but you won't find truffles for sale except in the priciest and most selective gourmet shops. Just recently an unusually large white Alba truffle, unearthed in Italy and weighing more than four pounds, was auctioned at Sotheby's in New York City for $61,250. That's probably worth more than my house and definitely tastes a whole helluva lot better.

Watermelon-Jalapeño Ice Pops

{MAKES ABOUT 2 DOZEN POPS}

TALK ABOUT PURE SUMMER on a stick! These ice pops are a beautiful pink color, sweet, and spicy. Just right for a summer afternoon. Use this recipe as a jumping-off point to make other colorful ice pops. What about cucumber-mint? Tomato-basil? Carrot-ginger?

PREP TIME: **ABOUT 10 MINUTES**
COOKING TIME: **5 TO 7 MINUTES**

1 (2-pound) watermelon (seedless, if possible)

½ jalapeño, seeded and coarsely chopped

1 cup sugar

Salt

1. Scoop the watermelon flesh from the rind and remove the seeds. Cube the watermelon and put it in a large bowl. Add the jalapeño (no need to stir the mixture at this point).

2. In a saucepan, bring the sugar and 1 cup of water to a boil. Reduce the heat to medium and simmer until the sugar dissolves to make simple syrup. Let the syrup cool a little.

3. Pour the syrup over the watermelon and jalapeño. Transfer the mixture to the bowl of a food processor fitted with the metal blade, or a blender, and process until smooth. Season with salt and pulse again.

4. Strain the watermelon mixture through a double layer of cheesecloth into another bowl. Pour into ice pop molds and freeze until firm. The pops will keep in the freezer for up to a month.

Grilled Cheese Sliders with Pancetta and Tomato Marmalade {SERVES 2}

JUST ABOUT EVERYONE LIKES a grilled cheese sandwich; it oozes with warmth and flavor. I came up with these sliders as a new spin on the classic American combo of grilled cheese and tomato soup. I bumped up the flavor by using aged cheddar and salty pancetta, both deliciously highlighted by the sweet-and-sour tomato marmalade. If you'd rather make a more substantial sandwich, use supersoft potato bread; its natural sweetness works well with the sandwich's salty-sweet flavors.

PREP TIME: **ABOUT 20 MINUTES**
COOKING TIME: **23 TO 30 MINUTES**

TOMATO MARMALADE

- 1 tomato, diced
- ¼ cup chopped red onion
- 1 garlic clove, minced
- 2 tablespoons red wine vinegar
- 1 teaspoon honey
- Salt and freshly ground black pepper

SANDWICH

- 2 small potato rolls (1½ to 2 inches in diameter)
- 2 ounces sharp cheddar cheese, shredded (about ½ cup)
- 4 slices pancetta, large enough to nearly cover each half of the rolls (see Note)
- 2 tablespoons olive oil

1. For the marmalade, in a saucepan, mix the tomatoes with the onion and garlic. Cook over medium heat for 10 to 15 minutes, or until the tomatoes break down and start to resemble a sauce. Stir occasionally during cooking to prevent sticking and encourage even cooking.

2. Add the vinegar and honey and cook, stirring occasionally, for 5 to 6 minutes longer, or until the sauce thickens. Season to taste with salt and pepper.

3. Set the marmalade aside to cool. If not using right away, transfer to a container with a lid and refrigerate for up to 2 days.

4. Preheat the oven to 350°F.

5. Split the rolls, put them on a baking sheet, and sprinkle with the cheese. Put a slice of pancetta on top of the cheese in each roll and bake for about 5 minutes, or until the cheese has melted.

6. Remove the baking sheet from the oven and spread 2 tablespoons of the marmalade on one side of each cheese-and-pancetta-topped roll. Top with the other side of each roll so that the cheese is facing in.

7. One at a time, transfer the sandwiches to a panini press or hot frying pan set over medium-high heat (if using a frying pan, heat 2 tablespoons of oil in the pan first) and cook for about 3 minutes, or until the bread is golden brown and crunchy. If using a frying pan, turn the bread once during cooking so that both sides of the roll brown. Repeat with the other sandwich.

8. Cut the sandwiches in half and serve.

NOTE: Lots of folks don't think there's much difference between pancetta and bacon. True, you can usually substitute bacon for pancetta and get good results, but without question pancetta is worth seeking out. You'll be rewarded every time. The primary difference is that pancetta is not smoked. It's made from pork belly that's been rubbed with spices and then cured for two or three months. This makes it moister than our slab bacon and incredibly tasty.

What Exactly Is Marmalade?

Truth is, I can't answer my own question; there doesn't seem to be a precise definition for marmalade. If you look it up in books or Google it, the most consistent definition is that it's a citrus preserve that includes the fruit's rind. Classic orange marmalade—the flavor most of us think of when we say "marmalade" or that nasty English breakfast– or afternoon tea–inspired spread for room-temp toast—is best made with Seville oranges; spoonfuls of sugar compensate for the bitterness and the outcome is a seductive balance of sweet and bitter.

Of course, there's not an orange marmalade in sight in this book, but I've included three other marmalades on these pages. One is tomato-based, another made with onions, and the third with shallots. All are a little chunky, a little sweet, a little sour. You might call them "relish" or "chutney," but as they say, a marmalade by any other name would still taste as sweet and sour!

But what about the word? Chances are good that it derives from a Portuguese word for a kind of quince, quince being the original ingredient in marmalade. But I like an alternative explanation I came across out there on the Internet—unlikely as it is. In the sixteenth century, a French doctor was treating Mary, Queen of Scots, for seasickness, the story goes, and came up with a stomach-settling remedy of chopped oranges and sugar. The concoction was called *"Marie est malade."* See how that leads to "marmalade"? Wild! Even if you don't believe a word, I say keep the tale alive. It's a way cool story.

Seared Prawn Sliders {SERVES 2}

PRAWNS ARE THE BIGGER, meaner brother to the wee baby shrimp. Look at him (or cook him) the wrong way, and he'll kick your ass after school! Being more ripped and stronger than shrimp, these guys can take some extra time to cook, which in this case means more time searing. Basically, searing is the same as sautéing, but with higher heat so you get better caramelization on the food. Put the burly prawns between some sweet bread and slide 'em away, good to go.

PREP TIME: 8 TO 10 MINUTES, PLUS SOAKING
COOKING TIME: ABOUT 5 MINUTES

½ cup rice wine vinegar

½ cup sugar

½ cup finely diced pineapple

4 sprigs cilantro, chopped

½ avocado, peeled

2 teaspoons fresh lime juice

Salt and freshly ground black pepper

2 teaspoons soy sauce

2 tablespoons mayonnaise

6 large prawns, shelled and halved lengthwise

4 small sweet Hawaiian rolls or potato rolls (each about 3 inches in diameter)

2 tablespoons canned wasabi peas, crushed

2 tablespoons minced red onion

1. In a small saucepan, heat the vinegar and sugar over medium heat until the sugar dissolves. Don't let the mixture boil.

2. Put the pineapple pieces in a glass or ceramic bowl and pour the warm vinegar over the fruit. Stir gently and then set aside for about 30 minutes. Discard the liquid. Stir the cilantro into the pineapple and set aside until needed.

3. In another bowl, mash the avocado with the lime juice and season with salt and pepper.

4. In a separate small bowl, stir the soy sauce with the mayonnaise to make soy aioli.

5. Heat a dry skillet over high heat and when hot, sear the prawns for about 30 seconds on all sides until nicely colored and just cooked through (don't overcook).

6. Spead the soy aioli on the rolls and then divide the prawn halves among the rolls. Top with the avocado mash and then spoon the pineapple over the avocado. Garnish each slider with wasabi peas and red onion. Put the tops of the rolls in place and serve.

Smoked Salmon with Dill Schmear and Bagel Chips {SERVES 6}

CLOSE YOUR EYES AND TAKE A BITE. You'll immediately recognize the Sunday-morning flavors of bagels and lox, particularly if you've spent any time in New York. This has the same yum factor, but it's more fun to look at—almost like a bagel turned inside out. It's pretty as is, but you could dress it up even more with cherry tomatoes.

PREP TIME: **ABOUT 25 MINUTES**
COOKING TIME: **ABOUT 20 MINUTES**

½ cup sugar

¼ cup apple cider vinegar

1 red onion, thinly sliced

3 ounces capers

2 tablespoons canola oil

1 plain bagel

½ cup olive oil

Salt and freshly ground black pepper

8 ounces cream cheese

1 bunch dill, coarsely chopped

1½ pounds smoked salmon, thinly sliced

1. In a sauté pan, mix the sugar and vinegar with ½ cup of water and bring to a boil. Stir in the onion, reduce the heat to medium-low, and simmer for about 5 minutes, or until the mixture thickens to the consistency of marmalade. Set aside.

2. Drain the capers and rinse them under cool running water. Pat them dry with paper towels. In a saucepan, heat the canola oil and when hot, fry the capers for about 2 minutes, or until crispy. Set the capers aside.

3. Preheat the oven to 350°F.

4. Using a serrated knife, slice the bagel crosswise into thin slices, keeping the shape of the bagel.

5. Lay the bagel slices on baking sheets and drizzle with the olive oil. Season lightly with salt and pepper. Bake for about 10 minutes, or until golden brown and crispy. Do not turn them during baking. Remove the bagel chips from the baking sheets and set aside to cool.

6. In the bowl of a food processor fitted with the metal blade, combine the cream cheese and dill and pulse until smooth.

7. Spoon about 1 tablespoon of the dill cream cheese in the center of each of six serving plates. Top the cream cheese with some of the onion marmalade. Arrange slices of the salmon around the center of the plate and put a bagel chip on each plate. Garnish with the crispy capers and serve.

Peppercorn-Crusted Ahi Tuna with Parmesan Crisps {SERVES 4}

THIS IS A PLAY ON A CLASSIC chicken Caesar salad, made with romaine, anchovies, and plenty of garlic. In place of chicken, I serve peppercorn-crusted ahi tuna, which elevates it several notches above a chicken Caesar. The only tricky part is making the crisps—and they aren't hard. Use a ring mold if that helps, or make them freehand as I explain here. The trick is to create a thin of layer of cheese that has no gaps. If there are gaps, the tiny pieces of grated cheese won't melt into one another and form an all-important bond. If the cheese is spread too thick, the crisps will be "chews." How successful you are depends on your level of experience. With a little practice, you'll be a superstar.

PREP TIME: **ABOUT 25 TO 30 MINUTES**
COOKING TIME: **ABOUT 1 HOUR**

4 ounces Parmesan cheese, grated (about 1 cup)

1 whole head garlic

8 anchovy fillets, packed in oil

1 cup fish stock

Salt and freshly ground black pepper

8 tablespoons (1 stick) unsalted butter

4 pieces tuna, each cut into a log and weighing about 3 ounces

¼ cup finely ground pink peppercorns (see Note)

2 hearts of romaine, leaves separated

Leaves from 4 sprigs chervil, for garnish

1. Preheat the oven to 350°F. Line a baking sheet with parchment paper or a Silpat.

2. To make 4 tuiles, pat the cheese into 4 circles, each about 2½ inches in diameter, directly on the parchment or Silpat. Bake for 5 to 7 minutes, or until the cheese melts together and the tuiles are golden brown.

3. Using a thin metal spatula, lift the tuiles from the baking sheet and set aside on plates to cool. They can also cool on the pan if they seem too difficult to move to plates. Do not turn off the oven.

4. Cut the head of garlic in half crosswise through the center (equator). Wrap the garlic halves in a single piece of foil and bake for 30 to 45 minutes, or until tender and golden brown. Unwrap the garlic and when cool enough to handle, peel off the papery skin.

5. Transfer the garlic to a blender and add the anchovies and fish stock. Blend until smooth. Season with salt and pepper and then strain through a fine-mesh sieve into a saucepan. Bring to a simmer over medium heat. Add the butter and cook, stirring, until the butter melts and emulsifies the sauce.

6. Season the tuna with salt and pepper. Heat a nonstick skillet over high heat and when hot, sear the tuna logs for about 10 seconds on all sides. (If the tuna sticks, add a drizzle of olive oil.)

7. Spread the peppercorns on a plate and roll the logs in them to coat. Set aside.

8. Put 3 pieces of romaine in the center of each of four bowls. Thinly slice the tuna and arrange the slices on top of the lettuce. Put a tuile on top of the tuna on each plate.

9. Using an immersion blender, froth the garlic-anchovy emulsion and spoon the froth over the tuna and tuiles. Garnish each serving with chervil.

NOTE: A coffee or spice grinder works perfectly to grind the peppercorns.

Buffalo Chicken with Celery Slaw and Blue Cheese {SERVES 6}

THIS WAS A HIT when I put it on the opening menu at Graham Elliot Bistro in Chicago (my first restaurant), and it stays on the menu by popular demand. I like chicken thighs because of their full flavor, but chicken breasts are tasty, too. Or keep it traditional and cook up some wings. Whatever part of the chicken you choose, keep the skin on; it's what gets crispy. At the restaurant, we usually deep-fry the roulades of chicken, but it's easier to panfry them as I describe here. If you're into deep-frying, have a go at it!

I've taken liberties with tradition. The blue cheese shows up as a fondant with sour cream and mustard. I make a mustardy celery slaw with celery root as well as celery stalks and leaves. Finally, the beer bubbles are fun but not necessary. They're easy to make but do require xanthan gum and powdered soy lecithin, as well as a powerful blender. You might decide to pop open a can of cold beer and drink it instead!

PREP TIME: **ABOUT 40 MINUTES**
COOKING TIME: **ABOUT 25 MINUTES**

BLUE CHEESE FONDANT

- 6 ounces Wisconsin blue cheese or your favorite blue cheese, crumbled (about 1½ cups)
- ½ cup sour cream
- 1 teaspoon Dijon mustard
- ¼ teaspoon Tabasco
- ¼ teaspoon Worcestershire sauce
- 1 teaspoon fresh lemon juice
- Salt

CHICKEN

- 6 boneless, skin-on chicken thighs or breasts
- Coarse salt and freshly cracked black pepper
- 3 to 4 tablespoons canola oil
- ¼ cup thinly sliced onions
- 1 garlic clove, thinly sliced
- ½ cup Frank's Hot Sauce (or a similar hot sauce)
- 1 teaspoon Sriracha
- 1 tablespoon distilled white vinegar
- 8 tablespoons (1 stick) cold unsalted butter, cut into pieces
- Fresh lemon juice (optional)
- Celery Slaw and reserved celery leaves (recipe follows)
- Beer Bubbles (recipe follows), optional

1. For the fondant, in a blender, puree the blue cheese, sour cream, and mustard until smooth. Add the Tabasco, Worcestershire sauce, and lemon juice and blend until mixed. Season with salt. Refrigerate until needed.

2. For the chicken, open the thighs as flat as you can, pressing on the meat with your hands. If using breasts, lay them flat on the work surface. The meat should lie on the countertop, skin side down. Season both sides with salt and pepper. Roll the meat into roulades, or rolls, and tie the ends and center with kitchen twine. This is to promote even cooking.

3. Bring a large pot of lightly salted water to a boil over medium-high heat. Reduce the heat to maintain a simmer and poach the chicken for 18 to 20 minutes, or until fully cooked. The cooking time will depend on the size of the rolls and how tightly they are rolled.

4. When cooked, transfer the chicken to a large bowl filled with cold water and ice cubes to cool completely.

5. In a skillet, heat 2 to 3 tablespoons of the oil over medium-high heat, and when hot, panfry the roulades for 2 to 3 minutes so that the skin crisps up.

6. In a saucepan, heat the remaining oil over medium heat. When hot, cook the onions and garlic, stirring, until caramelized and a rich amber color. Add the hot sauce, Sriracha, vinegar, and ¼ cup of water. Let the sauce come to a simmer and cook for about 10 minutes, or until the flavors blend into a full-bodied sauce.

7. Transfer the sauce to a blender and puree until smooth. With the blender running, add the butter, a piece at a time, until incorporated and smooth. Season with salt and a little lemon juice, if using.

8. Slice each roulade into 3 wheels. Discard the twine. Carefully toss the sliced chicken with the buffalo sauce to coat evenly on all sides.

9. Spoon 2 to 4 tablespoons of the slaw in the center of each of six plates. Put 3 slices of chicken on top of the slaw.

10. Garnish each plate with blue cheese fondant, beer bubbles, and the reserved celery leaves from the following recipe for celery slaw.

Celery Slaw {MAKES ABOUT 2 CUPS}

PREP TIME: ABOUT 10 MINUTES, PLUS CHILLING

½ cup sour cream

2 tablespoons distilled white vinegar

1 tablespoon whole-grain mustard

1 tablespoon mayonnaise

1 teaspoon honey

1 teaspoon celery seeds

1 teaspoon Tabasco

2 celery stalks, cut into thin slices, leaves reserved for garnish

1 small celery root (celeriac), peeled and julienned (see Note)

1 tablespoon chopped flat-leaf parsley

½ tablespoon minced shallot

Juice of 1 lemon

Salt

1. In a large bowl, stir the sour cream, vinegar, mustard, mayonnaise, honey, celery seeds, and Tabasco. Gently fold in the sliced celery, celery root, parsley, and shallot. Season to taste with lemon juice and salt.

2. Refrigerate the slaw for about 2 hours to allow the flavors to come together. Take it from the refrigerator about 15 minutes before serving to bring to room temperature.

NOTE: Celery root is also called celeriac. It's not the root of the same celery plant that produces the familiar stalks—it's the root of a related celery plant and works with my idea of serving the "whole" veg.

Beer Bubbles {MAKES ABOUT 12 OUNCES}

PREP TIME: ABOUT 15 MINUTES
COOKING TIME: ABOUT 5 MINUTES

1 (12-ounce) can Pabst Blue Ribbon beer, your favorite beer, or what you have on hand

1 tablespoon sugar

Squeeze of fresh lemon juice

1 teaspoon xanthan gum

2 tablespoons powdered soy lecithin

1. In a saucepan, bring the beer to a gentle simmer and cook for about 5 minutes to cook off the alcohol. Stir in the sugar and a squeeze of lemon juice. Remove from the heat and let the beer cool.

2. When cool, transfer the beer to a high-powered blender (such as Vitamix) and with the motor running, slowly add the xanthan gum. Pour the beer into a deep bowl or pan.

3. Using an immersion blender, blend the soy lecithin into the beer to create bubbles.

FEELING HOT, HOT, HOT!

When Christopher Columbus set out to find the far-flung Spice Islands, he got more than he bargained for on the Caribbean island of Hispaniola (Haiti and the Dominican Republic). He would find, among other foodstuffs, chiles, potatoes, tomatoes, and squash. (And chocolate, God bless 'im!) Understandably, the Europeans tended to think of the chiles in terms of heat, not flavor.

Today we're more apt to recognize different flavors among the hundreds of chiles now grown all over the world, although we also register heat. (How could we not?) These flavors are apparent in hot sauces, if you take the time to taste them. And clearly, many, many people have taken the time. There's an explosion of hot sauces from coast to coast and plenty of customers for each and every one. Some hot sauces are made by small companies and sold regionally; others are bottled by big companies and are available just about everywhere.

That's why I specify different hot sauces throughout the book. Some, like Crystal hot sauce, are mild and fruity, while Tapatío packs a little more raw heat. The ever-popular Sriracha boasts a little sweetness with its heat. Tabasco is not so much a sauce as an acidic peppery flavoring. Frank's is straightforward and about as hot as most folks like. You can find fiery hot sauces that set your tongue quivering, if that's what you want, and you can find others that are warm and peppery with mild heat. Experiment and discover what you like. Look for both flavor and heat—not heat alone.

Crispy Prosciutto-Wrapped Figs with Ricotta {MAKES 12}

THIS IS A NO-BRAINER, and it also happens to be a dish we used to do at the Chicago restaurant TRU, where I worked with the amazing chef Rick Tramonto. Omit the prosciutto and simply grill fresh figs for some of that smokiness to make it vegetarian (if you're into that kinda thing).

PREP TIME: **ABOUT 15 MINUTES**
COOKING TIME: **2 TO 3 MINUTES**

12 fresh figs

12 strips prosciutto (each about 4 inches long and 1 inch wide), fat trimmed

Olive oil

8 ounces sheep's-milk ricotta or other high-quality ricotta, drained (about 1 cup)

2 tablespoons honey

1 teaspoon ground sumac

1 teaspoon salt

1 teaspoon freshly ground black pepper

1. Wrap each fig in a strip of prosciutto and fasten closed with a toothpick.

2. Coat a skillet with a good film of oil, about ¼ inch deep, and heat over medium-high heat. Working in batches, sauté the wrapped figs on all sides for 2 to 3 minutes, or until the prosciutto is crispy. As each fig is cooked, transfer to a plate lined with paper towels.

3. In a small bowl, whisk the ricotta, honey, and sumac. Season with the salt and pepper.

4. Serve the figs with the ricotta sauce.

Prosciutto: Parma's Proud Ham If you haven't tried prosciutto, you have not lived! Put this book down and grab some ASAP. There are only three ingredients needed to make prosciutto—pork, salt, and time—and when they come together, magic happens. The real thing comes from Parma, in the Emilia-Romagna region of Italy, although very good prosciutto is made elsewhere these days. To make prosciutto, ham is neither smoked nor cooked, but instead is seasoned, salt-cured, and then air-dried. The process makes it edible with no cooking and results in some of the best-tasting meat anywhere. Buy it sliced very thin, ideally by a butcher while you wait, because the minute it's cut from the ham, it starts losing flavor. Plan to eat it the day you buy it. It's intense, for sure, so a little goes a long way. It's good with sweet fruits such as melon, pears, and figs.

Short Rib Tacos with Pickled Onions and Guacamole {SERVES 6}

WHEN YOU MAKE THE SHORT RIBS on page 161, you'll have bits and pieces left over. Use them in these awesome little tacos. They're rich and yummy with guacamole and lively with pickled onions. Or, if you don't have leftover short ribs, start from scratch. For a tropical beachy variation, forget the guac and serve with a mango salsa (see page 123) instead.

PREP TIME: **50 TO 60 MINUTES, PLUS CHILLING**
COOKING TIME: **ABOUT 6 HOURS**

SHORT RIBS

2 pounds short ribs

Salt

2 tomatoes, quartered and diced

1 large onion, cut into medium dice

1 head garlic, cloves separated and peeled but left whole

1 bunch cilantro, chopped

1 jalapeño, seeded and diced

1 tablespoon tomato paste

PICKLED ONIONS

1 large red onion, thinly sliced

½ cup apple cider vinegar

½ teaspoon salt

½ teaspoon dried oregano

¼ teaspoon cumin seeds

¼ teaspoon freshly cracked black pepper

GUACAMOLE

3 ripe avocados, peeled and chopped into large chunks

¼ cup diced onions

¼ cup chopped cilantro

½ teaspoon minced garlic

1 tablespoon chopped serrano chile

1 tablespoon fresh lime juice

1½ teaspoons salt

TACOS

Canola oil

12 (4-inch) tortillas (corn or flour, depending on your preference)

1. For the short ribs, sprinkle both sides of the ribs with salt and put them in the pot of a large slow cooker.

2. Add the tomatoes, onion, garlic cloves, cilantro, jalapeño, and tomato paste. Season well with about another tablespoon of salt and add 8 cups of water.

3. Cover and cook on medium-high heat for 6 hours, or until the meat is fall-off-the-bone tender.

4. For the pickled onions, put the onion slices in a large saucepan and add enough cold water to cover by an inch or so. Bring to a boil over medium-high heat and as soon as the water boils, remove the saucepan from the heat. Let the onions sit in the hot water for 5 minutes.

5. Drain the onions and transfer them to a tall, narrow jar that will hold them comfortably.

6. Add the vinegar, salt, oregano, cumin seeds, and pepper. Fill the jar with water, cover with a lid, and refrigerate for at least 5 hours. The pickles can be made up to 1 week ahead.

7. Remove the meat from the slow cooker and set aside on a platter. When cool enough to handle, pull the meat from the bones and discard the bones. Set the meat aside.

8. Transfer the contents of the slow cooker to a blender. Process until pureed to make the salsa for the tacos.

9. For the guacamole, put the avocados, onion, cilantro, garlic, serrano chile, lime juice, and salt in a medium bowl. With a spoon, mash the ingredients together to make a chunky salsa. Taste and adjust the seasoning.

10. For the tacos, transfer the meat from the short ribs to a saucepan. Add a little of the salsa and heat over medium heat until hot.

11. In a large frying pan, heat about 1 teaspoon of oil over medium heat and when hot, cook a tortilla for about 30 seconds on each side, until supple and warm. Repeat with all the tortillas, using more oil as needed.

12. Divide the warm meat among the tortillas and top with some salsa, pickled onions, and guacamole. Serve immediately.

Chorizo Meatballs with Spicy Tomato Sauce

{SERVES 6 TO 8; MAKES ABOUT 20 MEATBALLS}

CHORIZO IS SPICY AND SMOKY, two things that mankind has been drawn to for millennia. The tomato sauce isn't too hot and tends to balance well with the natural sweetness from the tomatoes themselves, but you can add or take away some of that heat, if you prefer. Making meatballs at home is fun and a good way to get the kids involved in the kitchen. Meatballs are also a perfect way to use up any leftover trimmings you have from beef, chicken, lamb, or pork.

PREP TIME: **ABOUT 20 MINUTES**
COOKING TIME: **40 TO 45 MINUTES**

MEATBALLS

3 tablespoons olive oil

1 small onion, diced

2 garlic cloves, minced

8 ounces ground pork shoulder

8 ounces lean ground beef

2 Spanish chorizo sausages, casings removed, sausage meat minced

2 large eggs

2 ounces Parmesan cheese, grated (about ½ cup)

½ cup dried bread crumbs

¼ cup red wine

1 tablespoon chopped flat-leaf parsley

1½ teaspoons minced fresh chives

1 teaspoon piment d'Espelette, cayenne pepper, or hot paprika

1 teaspoon ground sumac

Grated zest of 1 lemon

Salt

SPICY TOMATO SAUCE

2 (14½-ounce) cans diced tomatoes, drained

1 (14½-ounce) can piquillo peppers, drained

¼ cup olive oil

3 garlic cloves, smashed

1 tablespoon harissa paste

2 tablespoons sherry vinegar

Fresh lemon juice

Salt

GARNISH

6 ounces feta cheese, crumbled (about 1½ cups)

2 tablespoons chopped flat-leaf parsley

2 tablespoons chopped mint leaves

1. For the meatballs, in a large skillet, heat about 2 tablespoons of the oil over medium-high heat. When hot, sauté the onion and garlic until the onion is translucent and softened. Set aside to cool.

2. Preheat the oven to 350°F.

3. In a large bowl, mix the pork, beef, sausage, eggs, Parmesan, bread crumbs, wine, parsley, chives, piment d'Espelette, sumac, lemon zest, and a little salt. Add the cooled onion and garlic. Using your hands, work the mixture until the ingredients are well mixed. Season with salt.

4. Roll the meat between your palms to make 20 small meatballs, about the size of walnuts.

5. In another large skillet, heat the remaining oil. You only need a film of oil to coat the skillet. Brown the meatballs on all sides and transfer to a baking sheet. Bake for about 15 minutes, or until cooked through.

6. Meanwhile, for the sauce, in a blender, puree the tomatoes, peppers, oil, garlic, and harissa. Transfer to a saucepan and bring to a boil. Reduce the heat and simmer for about 15 minutes, until the sauce has reduced by about one-third. Stir in the vinegar and season with lemon juice and salt.

7. Put the meatballs in the sauce and simmer for 3 to 4 minutes.

8. Garnish with the feta, parsley, and mint and serve.

The Beauty of Bread Crumbs

Okay, okay. Bread crumbs are pretty uninteresting. No. Revise that. They're boring. But despite their dullness, they are essential. I use them all the time for panfrying, deep-frying, and coating oven-baked food.

You can either buy bread crumbs or make your own. I don't much like the store-bought version, but I understand that sometimes you gotta do what you gotta do. Still, making them at home is easy, and when I call for "fresh" bread crumbs, you have to make them yourself. Just take a slice from a loaf of normal-size sandwich bread and rip it into large pieces. Process in a blender or food processor. Done! One slice yields about ½ cup of bread crumbs.

If you want to make dried bread crumbs—and unless I specify "fresh," the bread crumbs used in this book are all dried, i.e., toasted—lay slices of bread on a baking sheet and let them dry out in a 200°F oven for about an hour. Any hotter and the bread will brown—which is fine, if you want a crispier texture. Fresh bread crumbs keep in the refrigerator for three to four days and dried bread crumbs keep for about a month if refrigerated in an airtight container.

If you want panko bread crumbs, you have to buy them; you can't make these at home. Originally imported from Japan, these fragile, pointy crumbs are especially light and crunchy when used as a coating on fried food.

2

HOT SOUPS and COOL SALADS

IF THERE'S ANYTHING I'm known for, it's my ability to make yummy soups and salads. In this chapter, you'll get an idea of my thinking behind each offering, and I hope I can inspire you to put your own personal stamp on them.

When it comes to soup, I love the textures they deliver, be they bisques or chowders. Soups can be hearty, light, creamy, smooth, chunky, or a mix of all the above (not literally, but you get my point). And while we mostly think of soups as being hot, I am a big fan of cold soups, too.

Same thinking goes for the salads—textures and flavors run the gamut and rule the day. Salads perfectly capture the season because to achieve greatness, all you have to do is let the simplest but perfectly ripe ingredients speak for themselves. At the end of the day, a cook's or chef's sole job is to make things tasty, to get that tomato to taste like the greatest, most life-changing tomato of all time: add a little sea salt and a crack of black peppercorns, drizzle with some fruity olive oil, and scatter some torn basil from the garden on the plate. Keep this in mind when you're working through this cookbook, and this chapter especially. Remember the golden rule of "less is more."

Baked Potato Bisque with Wisconsin Cheddar and Candied Bacon {SERVES 6}

THIS SOUP IS FOR ANYONE who likes buttery baked potatoes. Raise your hands! The cheddar, bacon, and chive marshmallows make it extra yummy, and then the milk smooths it out. I use whole milk, but for a slightly lighter soup, substitute low-fat milk; for richer soup, use half-and-half. You could use pancetta instead of bacon. When home-cured with a little sugar, the pancetta is incredibly tasty.

PREP TIME: **ABOUT 20 MINUTES**
COOKING TIME: **35 TO 40 MINUTES**

CANDIED BACON

4 ounces bacon, diced

¼ cup sugar

POTATO BISQUE

8 leeks

2 tablespoons unsalted butter

2 pounds Yukon Gold potatoes, peeled, sliced, and soaked in cold water

3 cups whole milk

Salt and freshly ground black pepper

4 ounces four-year-old Wisconsin cheddar cheese or similar cheddar, grated (about 1 cup)

Chive Marshmallows (recipe follows), optional

1. For the candied bacon, in a large skillet, slowly cook the bacon over medium to medium-low heat until crispy and the fat has rendered. Drain the fat from the pan and sprinkle the sugar over the bacon.

2. Stir to coat all the pieces and cook for 1 to 2 minutes longer so that the sugar has time to melt and adhere to the bacon.

3. Using tongs, transfer the bacon to a small tray lined with parchment paper. Let cool until ready to use.

4. For the potato bisque, trim the leeks at both ends, removing most of the green part and the root end of the white. Soak them in plenty of cool water to remove any sand and grit. Slice the leeks crosswise into ¾- to 1-inch pieces.

5. In a large saucepan, melt the butter over medium-high heat. When hot, add the leeks and cook, stirring, for about 15 minutes, or until softened.

6. Drain the potatoes and add them to the saucepan with the milk. Bring the milk to a boil and then immediately lower the heat and simmer for 15 to 18 minutes longer, or until the potatoes are easily pierced with a small knife or a fork.

7. Working in batches, transfer the soup to a blender and puree until smooth. As each batch is pureed, pour it into a clean pot or bowl. Strain the soup through a fine-mesh sieve or chinois to make it smoother, if desired. Season with salt and pepper.

8. If necessary, gently reheat the soup and then ladle it into bowls. Top each bowl with some cheddar, candied bacon, and, if desired, a chive marshmallow.

Chive Marshmallows

{MAKES ONE 9 X 13-INCH PAN OF MARSHMALLOWS}

PREP TIME: 15 TO 20 MINUTES, PLUS SOAKING AND DRYING
COOKING TIME: ABOUT 5 MINUTES

Flavorless vegetable oil or cooking spray

3 tablespoons powdered gelatin

1 cup granulated sugar

⅓ cup light corn syrup

½ cup minced fresh chives

3 tablespoons dried chives

Confectioners' sugar, for coating

1. Line a shallow rimmed baking pan with plastic wrap. Rub neutral vegetable oil over the plastic wrap or spray it lightly with cooking spray.

2. In the bowl of a stand mixer fitted with the whisk attachment, sprinkle the gelatin over ¼ cup of cold water and set aside to soak for about 10 minutes.

3. In a small saucepan, combine the granulated sugar and corn syrup with ¼ cup of water and bring to a boil. Cook at a rapid boil for 1 minute.

4. With the mixer on high speed, slowly pour the hot sugar mixture over the gelatin. When mixed, use a silicone spatula to scrape the hot syrup onto the lined baking pan and smooth the surface so the syrup is spread evenly.

5. Set the marshmallows aside to dry for at least 1 hour, longer if you have the time.

6. Use a small, round cookie or biscuit cutter dipped in cold water to cut the marshmallows into small rounds about 1 inch in diameter. For a more rustic look, cut them into slightly larger squares. The marshmallows will be a little tacky.

7. Grind the fresh and dried chives in a spice grinder until very fine and spread on a flat dish. Spread the confectioners' sugar in another dish.

8. Roll the marshmallows in the chopped chives and then in the sugar. Alternatively, sprinkle the marshmallows with the sugar. Set on a baking sheet lined with parchment paper until ready to serve.

HOMEMADE MARSHMALLOWS

Marshmallows, you say? Yes. They're easy once you get over a fear of sugar cookery—which isn't a silly fear. Most chefs have scarred hands and wrists, and a number of those scars can be traced to hot sugar. The secret is to work deliberately—neither rushing nor languishing—and take care with the hot sugar because, well . . . it's hot! I suggest you use thick oven mitts and long-handled utensils. And stand as far back as you can when pouring the hot sugar syrup into the bowl with the gelatin.

I like to garnish hot soups with marshmallows. As they're stirred into the soup, they soften and dissolve, delivering a little sweetness as well as flavor. (You've done this with packaged marshmallows and a cup of hot cocoa.) For the bisque on page 40, the chive-coated marshmallows infuse the soup with sweetness and the taste of chives. I've paired cinnamon marshmallows with carrot bisque, lavender with pea soup, and cilantro with corn bisque. You could buy a bag of Jet-Puffed mini marshmallows and roll them in chives and confectioners' sugar or other flavors, but it wouldn't be the same.

Kabocha Squash Soup with Toasted Pepitas {SERVES 6}

EVERY BITE OF THIS SOUP tastes like autumn. Kabocha squash is so satisfying because of its rich squash-i-ness—and I like that it's not as well known as butternut and acorn squashes. Plus, it's fun to say. You can use another fall squash for the soup, but whatever you use, puree only half and then mix the chunkier half with the smooth half. The pepita garnish is a little time-consuming but extremely tasty. Make it when the in-laws are on their way over and you want to impress. But if you're eating the soup in your sweatpants, just toast some pepitas instead!

PREP TIME: **15 TO 20 MINUTES**
COOKING TIME: **30 TO 35 MINUTES**

TOASTED PEPITA-COCONUT-LIME GARNISH

¼ cup pepitas (pumpkin seeds)

1½ teaspoons canola oil

¼ cup shredded unsweetened coconut

¼ cup diced raw kabocha squash

1 teaspoon yuzu juice (see page 46)

Salt

1 lime

SOUP

1 tablespoon canola oil

2 lemongrass stalks, trimmed, gently bruised, and sliced (see Note)

1 small onion, sliced

2 tablespoons chopped fresh ginger

3 garlic cloves, chopped

3 red kabocha squash, peeled, seeded, and coarsely chopped

1 gallon vegetable broth, preferably homemade

1 tablespoon fresh lime juice

1 tablespoon salt, plus more as needed

1. For the pepita-coconut-lime garnish, preheat the oven to 325°F.

2. Toss the pepitas with the oil and spread them on a rimmed baking sheet. Toast in the oven for about 6 minutes, stirring once or twice to encourage even browning. Transfer to a cool plate to stop the cooking. Keep the oven on.

3. Spread the coconut on a rimmed baking sheet and toast in the oven for about 10 minutes, or until browned around the edges. Transfer to a cool plate.

4. In a small bowl, toss the squash with the yuzu juice and season with salt.

5. Grate the zest from the lime or peel and chop it. Peel the pith from the lime and slice the lime into thin rounds.

6. For the soup, in a stockpot, heat the oil over medium-high heat. When hot, add the lemongrass, onion, and ginger and cook, stirring, for about 1 minute, or until they soften slightly. Add the garlic and continue to stir for another minute or so until softened. Take care that the garlic does not burn.

7. Add the squash and the vegetable broth. The broth should cover the squash by about ½ inch—if not, add a little water. Let the broth come to a gentle boil and then reduce the heat and simmer for about 20 minutes, or until the squash is tender when pierced with a fork.

8. Working in batches and using a slotted spoon, transfer the squash and other vegetables to a blender in small, manageable amounts. Puree until smooth and add liquid from the pot to adjust the consistency.

9. As each batch of soup is pureed, transfer it to a clean pot. Add the lime juice and salt and stir to mix. Taste and adjust the seasoning, if necessary. Serve garnished with the toasted pepitas, coconut, squash, lime zest, and lime rounds.

NOTE: To bruise the lemongrass, put the stalks beneath the flat side of a large knife, such as a chef's knife, and use the heel of your hand or end of your fist to hit the knife. Don't hit too hard; you don't want to damage the lemongrass. Light bruising releases essential oils, which heighten the flavor. It's a technique used most often with herbs, spices, garlic, onions, and similar ingredients.

What's Yuzu?

Yuzu juice is sold bottled in most Japanese markets, many specialty markets, and online. It's the juice of a Japanese fruit that is rarely found outside of its island nation. The juice is sweetly sour and a little flowery, and while it's tough to describe to the uninitiated, many say it tastes like a mixture of lemons, grapefruit, and tangerines. If you can't find it, substitute fresh lemon or lime juice, but try for the yuzu. You won't be sorry!

Chilled Cucumber Gazpacho with Red Onions, Green Apples, and Mint {SERVES 4}

THE KEY WORD FOR THIS SOUP is "refreshing." Along with the cukes is the clean flavor of mint and the sweet-sour dynamic provided by the apples. There's a little sunshine in every bite of the beautiful gazpacho. You could almost drink it from a glass rather than eat it with a spoon, and after you eat it, you feel healthy and, as I said, refreshed! What's better?

PREP TIME: **ABOUT 10 MINUTES, PLUS MARINATING**

SOUP

- 3 English cucumbers
- ½ cup coarsely chopped red onion
- 3 sprigs fresh mint
- 1 garlic clove
- Salt
- ¼ cup coarsely chopped Granny Smith apple
- 1 teaspoon fresh lemon juice

GARNISH

- ¼ cup finely diced Granny Smith apple
- ¼ cup finely diced red onion
- ¼ teaspoon fresh lemon juice
- 10 fresh mint leaves, torn
- Salt

1. For the soup, halve the cucumbers lengthwise and coarsely chop them. Put them in a bowl with the onions, mint sprigs, garlic, and a sprinkling of salt. Cover the bowl and let the vegetables marinate for about 1 hour. Remove and discard the mint and garlic.

2. Put the cucumbers, onions, and apples in the bowl of a food processor fitted with the metal blade and pulse until the soup takes on the consistency of a granita (fluid but granular). Season with the lemon juice and salt.

3. For the garnish, mix the apples, onions, and lemon juice. Add the mint leaves, stir to combine, and season with salt.

4. Pour or ladle the soup into small bowls and top each with a small spoonful of the garnish right before serving.

Chilled Summer Cantaloupe Soup

{SERVES 6}

DEEP-ORANGE, RIPE CANTALOUPE is the star of this chilled soup, finally getting the respect it deserves. Too often the admirable melon is relegated to weary-looking fruit plates. What a shame; cantaloupes are a glory of nature. I always shop for them at farmers' markets, snatching them up when they smell musky and sweet. At that point you have a two-day window before the melon "goes off." When selecting cantaloupe or any other muskmelon, it's all about the aroma, not feel. Although if I have the choice, I like them when they still feel warm from the field.

PREP TIME: ABOUT 20 MINUTES

2 large ripe cantaloupes

1 cucumber

1 serrano chile

½ cup white verjus (see Note)

Juice of 2 limes

¼ cup extra-virgin olive oil, plus more for drizzling

3 tablespoons honey

Salt

1 cup slivered marcona almonds

1 cup sliced green grapes

1. Halve the cantaloupes, scoop out the seeds, and cut the melons into quarters. Peel the rind from the fruit and then chop the cantaloupe flesh into chunks. Transfer the fruit to a blender.

2. Peel the cucumber and halve it lengthwise. Scoop out the seeds (you won't get them all) and then chop the cucumber into chunks. Add to the blender with the cantaloupe.

3. Halve the chile and scrape out the seeds. Chop the chile and add it to the blender.

4. Puree the melon, cucumber, and chile until smooth. Add the verjus, lime juice, oil, and honey and pulse to mix.

5. Season with salt, pulse again, and pour into six bowls. Garnish each bowl with almonds and grapes and a drizzle of oil.

NOTE: Verjus is the juice of unripened white or red grapes. It's less acidic than vinegar, with a sweetly tart flavor that enhances sauces, salad dressings, and other preparations. Buy it in specialty stores or online. If you can't find it, substitute white wine vinegar.

Burrata, Tomato, and Olive Oil Crackers

{SERVES 4}

ONCE YOU TASTE BURRATA, ordinary mozzarella cheese pales into a distant memory. A good memory, sure, but not an outstanding one. What can compete with this smooth, rich buffalo- or cow's-milk cheese developed only in the last one hundred years in southern Italy? Similar to mozzarella on the outside, burrata is all creaminess on the inside—the name means "buttered." I pair it with summer's best tomatoes and fresh garden basil for a sassy, caprese-style salad that, in my opinion, can't be beat.

PREP TIME: ABOUT 10 MINUTES

8 fresh basil leaves, delicately torn, plus a handful of whole leaves for garnish

1 tablespoon chopped flat-leaf parsley

1 teaspoon chopped mint leaves

1 teaspoon grated lemon zest

1 garlic clove, thinly sliced

¼ cup extra-virgin olive oil

1 teaspoon fresh lemon juice

4 ripe tomatoes, preferably heirlooms, halved or quartered

1 pint ripe assorted cherry tomatoes, halved

Fleur de sel and freshly cracked black pepper

1 (12-ounce) ball burrata, drained (you can use smaller balls, but the weight should total about 12 ounces)

Olive Oil Crackers (page 53)

1. In a large bowl, mix the torn basil, parsley, mint, lemon zest, and garlic. Add the oil and lemon juice and whisk to combine. Gently toss the tomatoes in the dressing and season with fleur de sel and pepper. Let the tomatoes marinate for about 5 minutes.

2. Cut the burrata into thin slices and arrange them on four serving plates or a platter, if serving family style.

3. Lift the tomatoes from the dressing and arrange them around the burrata. Season with more salt and pepper and drizzle with the remaining dressing. Garnish with whole basil leaves.

4. Break the crackers into small shards with your hands. Serve the burrata and tomatoes with the crackers.

FLOUR POWER

In Italy, pasta is usually made with 00 or pasta flour, a relatively low-protein flour that produces perfect pasta with its desired "bite." The 00 designation doesn't refer to the percentage of protein in the flour, but instead to the fineness of the grind (Italian flours labeled 0, 1, or 2 are slightly more coarsely ground than 00). There are 00 flours with high percentages of protein that work beautifully for some breads and there are others with low percentages of protein that work best in pastries, so know what you're buying. For pasta (and the crackers on page 53), look for flour with 9.5 to 10 percent protein.

I like to mix all-purpose flour with 00 pasta flour when I make Olive Oil Crackers and similar baked goods. Much of the 00 flour sold in the United States has about the same percentages of protein as many of our all-purpose flours, which typically range from 10 to 11 percent, although the percentage of the 00 will be on the low side. So, if it's easier . . . go ahead and use good old, American-grown, all-purpose for the crackers—and for pasta and pizza, too, when you get right down to it.

But, if you're into discovery, pick up some 00 with similar or slightly lower percentages of protein than all-purpose and try it the next time you make these crackers or your own pasta dough. For a host of reasons—the wheat, the soil, the water, the air—the final result won't taste exactly as it did in Italy (or how your memory remembers it!), but the result will be darn good.

Whew! All this for crackers or pasta? If this seems over the top, turn to the all-purpose flour on the pantry shelf. You'll be okay.

Olive Oil Crackers {MAKES ABOUT 12 CRACKERS}

I SEPARATED THIS RECIPE from the burrata tomato salad (see page 50) because you'll want to make the crackers over and over again to serve with cheese, soups, and other salads. Or just to munch. Sure, you could easily buy some good crackers and call it a day, or you could even buy crackers and kick them up with a drizzle of olive oil and a sprinkling of salt followed by a warm-up in the oven.

Or you could make these. They're easy, and once they're baked, all you do is break them apart into shards.

PREP TIME: **15 MINUTES, PLUS RESTING**
COOKING TIME: **ABOUT 10 MINUTES**

¾ cup all-purpose flour, plus more for dusting

¾ cup 00 flour, pasta flour, or all-purpose flour

1 teaspoon kosher salt

3 tablespoons extra-virgin olive oil

1. In the bowl of a stand mixer fitted with the paddle attachment, mix the all-purpose flour, 00 flour, salt, oil, and ½ cup of warm water. When the dough comes together and forms a ball, remove it from the bowl and wrap it in plastic wrap. Refrigerate for at least 30 minutes and up to 24 hours.

2. When ready to bake, preheat the oven to 325°F. Line a baking sheet with parchment paper.

3. On a lightly floured surface, roll the dough to a thickness of about ⅛ inch or very thin.

4. Transfer the rolled dough to the lined baking sheet and prick it all over with the tines of a fork, which will keep the dough from bubbling too much (a little bubbling and swelling is fine). Bake for about 10 minutes, or until golden brown.

5. Let the cracker cool on a wire rack, then break into pieces to serve.

Graham's Signature Caesar Salad

{SERVES 4}

THIS SALAD IS AS CLOSE to a signature dish as I have, and it's been on my menus since 2004. The idea is to focus on the amazing texture and flavor of the oversized crouton. I call the crouton a "Twinkie" because that's exactly what it resembles, if Twinkies were filled with creamy cheese and garlic. Use brioche for the crouton, if you can, although any good, firm bread will do—as long as the loaf is not sliced.

I use a dressing based on *anchoïade*, a gutsy, anchovy and garlic–based sauce from the south of France. Its full-bodied herbaceousness makes a hard-to-miss statement, and being bright green, it's prettier than other dressings.

PREP TIME: **ABOUT 30 MINUTES**
COOKING TIME: **5 TO 7 MINUTES**

2 small heads romaine or romaine hearts

ANCHOÏADE DRESSING

2 tablespoons low-fat sour cream

2 tablespoons fresh lemon juice

1 tablespoon chopped shallot

1 teaspoon Dijon mustard

1 large egg yolk

2 garlic cloves, coarsely chopped

½ bunch flat-leaf parsley, coarsely chopped

3 ounces Parmesan cheese, grated (about ¾ cup)

1 cup grapeseed oil

1 teaspoon anchovy oil (from the can of anchovies) or extra-virgin olive oil

TWINKIE FILLING

3 ounces mascarpone cheese (about ¼ cup plus 2 tablespoons)

2 ounces cream cheese

2 ounces Parmesan cheese, grated (about ½ cup)

2 tablespoons half-and-half

½ tablespoon minced shallot

1 tablespoon minced garlic

Salt

BRIOCHE TWINKIES

½ unsliced brioche loaf or loaf of white bread

8 tablespoons (1 stick) unsalted butter

PARMESAN FLUFF

4 ounces Parmesan cheese

GARNISH

12 Spanish white anchovy fillets

Freshly ground black pepper

1. Trim the heads of romaine so the tops are somewhat even and discard the tough base. Cut the heads into quarters, to make 8 pieces total. Soak the lettuce quarters in cold water for a few minutes. Pat dry and set aside.

2. For the dressing, put the sour cream, lemon juice, shallot, mustard, egg yolk, garlic, and parsley in a blender and puree on high speed until smooth.

3. Add the Parmesan and puree for about 1 minute longer. With the blender running on medium speed, slowly add the grapeseed oil and anchovy oil in thin, steady streams. Pause every 10 seconds to make sure the oil is fully incorporated. If the dressing is too thick, add a touch of water.

4. For the Twinkie filling, in the bowl of a food processor fitted with the metal blade, mix the mascarpone, cream cheese, Parmesan, half-and-half, shallot, and garlic. Process until fully incorporated. Season with salt and pulse to mix.

5. Using a rubber spatula, transfer the filling to a pastry bag fitted with a plain tip and set aside.

6. For the brioche Twinkies, preheat the oven to 350°F.

7. Using a serrated knife, remove all the crust from the brioche loaf. Slice 8 rectangles from the loaf, each about 3 inches wide and 1 inch thick. (It's a good idea to cut a few extras, in case you need them.)

8. In a small saucepan, melt the butter. Brush the melted butter over all sides of the bread rectangles.

9. Heat a nonstick sauté pan over medium heat and gently brown the Twinkies on all sides.

10. Drain on paper towels to absorb any excess butter.

11. Use the rounded handle of a wooden spoon to hollow out two holes in the bottom of the Twinkies, each about ½ inch deep.

12. For the Parmesan fluff, using a Microplane, carefully grate the Parmesan over a bowl. The Microplane will produce very light, fluffy gratings. While you can grate the cheese ahead, grating it just before use will ensure it's light and fluffy.

13. To assemble the salad, use a clean paintbrush or similar brush to generously coat each piece of lettuce with dressing. Roll the coated lettuce in the fluff so all the pieces are nicely covered.

14. Meanwhile, pipe the filling in the holes in each Twinkie until stuffed. Put the filled Twinkies on a baking sheet and put in the oven for about 3 minutes to warm the centers. Remove from the oven.

15. Put 2 warm Twinkies on each of four serving plates and gently rest a piece of lettuce on top of each Twinkie. Garnish each plate with 3 anchovy fillets and season with pepper.

Olive Oil–Poached Tuna Niçoise {SERVES 6}

WHEN YOU TAKE THE TIME to confit tuna in olive oil, you end up with a substantial dish that is about as perfect as it gets when mixed with other traditionally Mediterranean ingredients. Making a confit is no more complicated than slowly cooking food in enough fat to cover—in this case, tuna in olive oil.

PREP TIME: **10 TO 15 MINUTES, PLUS MARINATING AND RESTING**
COOKING TIME: **ABOUT 10 MINUTES**

TUNA

- 1 pound albacore tuna
- Salt
- 2 cups olive oil
- 4 garlic cloves
- 2 bay leaves
- 2 tablespoons chopped flat-leaf parsley
- Grated zest of 1 lemon
- 1 tablespoon whole black peppercorns

SALAD

- 6 large eggs
- Salt
- 1 cup sliced haricots verts (1½-inch lengths)
- ½ cup pitted kalamata olives, rinsed and drained
- 2 garlic cloves, coarsely chopped
- 2 tablespoons chopped fresh basil
- 1 tablespoon chopped Spanish anchovies
- ¼ cup extra-virgin olive oil, plus 1 or 2 tablespoons to toss with the haricots verts
- 1 small loaf focaccia
- ½ cup Lemon Aioli (page 122)
- 1 large roasted red bell pepper (see page 58), seeded and coarsely chopped
- Juice of 1 lemon
- Freshly ground black pepper

1. For the tuna, season the fish with salt and put it in a large dish. Add the olive oil, garlic cloves, bay leaves, parsley, lemon zest, and peppercorns. Turn several times to coat the tuna on all sides with the oil and other ingredients. Cover and refrigerate for at least 3 hours and up to 8 hours or overnight.

2. Transfer the tuna and its marinade to a saucepan and bring to a simmer over low heat. Reduce the heat to very low and cook gently for about 7 minutes, or until the tuna is cooked through, with no red remaining.

3. Remove the saucepan from the heat and set aside, uncovered, for 30 minutes. The tuna will keep in the oil for up to 1 week if refrigerated. When ready to serve, remove the tuna from the oil.

4. For the salad, fill a saucepan with water and bring to a rapid boil. Gently add the eggs to the water using a long-handled spoon and cook for 2 minutes. Remove the pan from the heat and let the eggs sit in the hot water for at least 10 minutes to hard-cook them. Drain the eggs and run cold water over them until they are cool. Peel the eggs and set aside.

5. Fill a saucepan with heavily salted water and bring to a boil. While waiting for the water to boil, fill a metal bowl with cold water and ice cubes. Set the bowl near the sink. Put the beans in the boiling water and cook for 30 seconds. Drain and plunge the beans into the ice bath to cool. When cool, drain and pat dry with a clean dish towel or paper towels.

6. In the bowl of a food processor fitted with the metal blade, process the olives, garlic, basil, and anchovies until smooth. With the motor running, drizzle ¼ cup of the extra-virgin olive oil through the feed tube to help break down the tapenade. Transfer the tapenade to a bowl and fold in ½ cup of the aioli (you can save the remaining for 2 to 3 days in the fridge).

7. Slice the focaccia into 12 small slices, each ½ to ¼ inch thick. Lightly toast the bread.

8. Spread the olive tapenade–aioli mixture over the focaccia slices and crumble the tuna over it. Top with the peppers. Toss the haricots verts with the lemon juice, salt, pepper, and 1 to 2 tablespoons of extra-virgin olive oil and spoon over or around the tuna. Cut the eggs in half and serve alongside the tuna.

How to Roast a Bell Pepper Using a long-handled fork, hold the pepper over an open flame until all sides are charred. Alternatively, broil the pepper, turning it several times, until charred on all sides. Put the charred pepper in a plastic or paper bag and seal or fold it closed. Steam will build up in the bag, which helps loosen the charred skin. This will make it easier to peel. Once the pepper has cooled, rub off the skin with a clean dish towel or your fingers. Try to remove all the charred skin, but a few pieces left on the pepper makes no difference and adds to its charm.

Arugula Salad with Asian Pear and Roasted Beets {SERVES 4}

SOMETIMES SIMPLE IS BEST and this is a dish that showcases the concept. It focuses on the craft of cooking as opposed to the artistry, essentially being composed of three ingredients that are allowed to taste like themselves: arugula, pears, and beets. Buy the best.

PREP TIME: **ABOUT 12 MINUTES**
COOKING TIME: **ABOUT 30 MINUTES**

2 small golden beets	Salt and freshly ground black pepper
2 small red beets	1 Asian pear (see Note)
4 tablespoons olive oil	Fresh lemon juice
2 tablespoons sherry vinegar	4 ounces arugula (4 good handfuls)
1 shallot, minced	

1. Preheat the oven to 350°F.

2. Put the beets and 2 tablespoons of the oil in a bowl and toss to coat. Wrap the beets in aluminum foil and roast for about 30 minutes, or until tender when pierced with a fork. Unwrap the beets and set aside until cool enough to handle, then slip off their skins. Dice the beets into 1-inch cubes.

3. Whisk the remaining 2 tablespoons oil with the vinegar and shallot. Season with salt and pepper.

4. Core and julienne the Asian pear and put the slices in a bowl of cold water mixed with a little lemon juice (acidulated water) to keep them from turning brown and crisp them a little. Drain the pear just before using.

5. In a large bowl, toss the arugula with the beets and Asian pear. Drizzle the vinaigrette over the salad, toss gently, and season with salt and pepper.

NOTE: Dark yellow–skinned Asian pears are related to other pears but taste a little more like an apple. They are exceptionally juicy and are almost always served raw. They are also called Chinese pears or Japanese pears and should be sold carefully wrapped to prevent bruising.

Iceberg Wedge with Smoked Bacon and Roquefort Dressing {SERVES 4}

WHEN YOU PUT SOME LETTUCE underneath bacon and blue cheese, it's easier to rationalize eating those two rascals. And while arugula and field greens are more trendy, I like iceberg lettuce. It has great flavor and is super crisp, and deserves more love than being relegated to the space between the burger and the bun.

PREP TIME: **ABOUT 5 MINUTES**
COOKING TIME: **ABOUT 5 MINUTES**

2 heads iceberg lettuce, outer leaves removed if necessary

8 ounces unsliced smoked bacon

1 cup buttermilk

1 cup mayonnaise

2 ounces Roquefort cheese, crumbled (about ½ cup)

Leaves from 2 sprigs tarragon

Salt and freshly ground black pepper

4 Roma (plum) tomatoes or other ripe tomatoes, very thinly sliced

Freshly cracked black pepper

1. Quarter the heads of lettuce from stem to tip.

2. Chop the bacon into 1-inch square pieces and sauté in a skillet over medium heat until the fat has rendered. Using a slotted spoon, lift the bacon from the skillet and set aside on paper towels to cool and crisp up. Discard the fat.

3. In a small bowl, whisk the buttermilk, mayonnaise, ¼ cup of the cheese, and the tarragon. Season with salt and pepper.

4. Put 2 lettuce wedges on each of four salad plates. Arrange the tomato slices around the lettuce and scatter the bacon pieces over the lettuce and tomatoes. Drizzle the dressing over the lettuce and tomatoes. Finish with cracked black pepper and the remaining ¼ cup cheese.

Belgian Endive with Walnuts and Clementine Vinaigrette {SERVES 4}

I WAS SEVENTEEN when I got my first restaurant job as a dishwasher and had never heard of endive, much less seen it. When it arrived at the back door of the kitchen, I thought it was the coolest thing in the world. Nature had created this awesome-looking vegetable so delicate that each bullet-shaped head had to be wrapped in purple paper. Discovering it there in the restaurant kitchen was for me like Indiana Jones and the Ark of the Covenant.

Endive is a bitter veg, which can make it a hard sell to Americans, who have a sweet palate. In the rest of the world, bitterness is more appreciated. I dress the endive with a light dressing made from clementines, but if you want to make it more substantial, add an egg yolk and some mustard. You can also add some blue cheese, as they do in France for a similar salad.

PREP TIME: **ABOUT 5 MINUTES**
COOKING TIME: **7 TO 10 MINUTES**

1 cup coarsely chopped walnuts	¼ cup white wine vinegar
6 clementines	3 sprigs flat-leaf parsley, minced
¼ cup olive oil	Salt and freshly ground black pepper
¼ cup walnut oil	12 heads Belgian endive, halved lengthwise

1. Preheat the oven to 350°F.

2. Spread the walnuts on a rimmed baking sheet. Bake for 7 to 10 minutes, or until they darken a shade and are fragrant. Slide the nuts from the baking sheet onto a plate to cool.

3. Squeeze the juice from 2 clementines into a small bowl. Peel the remaining 4 clementines and divide them into segments. Mix the clementine juice with the olive and walnut oils and vinegar. Add the parsley, whisk well, and season with salt and pepper.

4. Arrange 6 endive halves in the center of each of four serving plates and top each with clementine segments (1 fruit for each serving). Drizzle the vinaigrette over the endive and top with the toasted walnuts.

Roasted Potato Salad {SERVES 4}

WHEN I THINK OF GOOD ol' potato salad—an American classic that shows up at every picnic, family reunion, and Fourth of July celebration—I like to take another route. Rather than boil the potatoes, I roast 'em to concentrate their earthy flavor. I look for purple, red skinned, Yukon Golds—any potatoes with different colors. It's a good way to draw the eye to this basic dish and helps get kids to try it.

PREP TIME: **10 MINUTES, PLUS CHILLING**
COOKING TIME: **40 TO 45 MINUTES**

2 pounds fingerling potatoes

3 garlic cloves

6 sprigs fresh thyme

1 bay leaf

1 tablespoon whole black peppercorns

2 tablespoons olive oil

1 cup mayonnaise (I like Hellmann's)

2 hard-cooked eggs, chopped

3 tablespoons diced red onion

2 tablespoons diced celery

1 tablespoon Dijon mustard

1 tablespoon chopped flat-leaf parsley

1 tablespoon chopped tarragon

1. Preheat the oven to 350°F.

2. In a large bowl, toss the potatoes with the garlic, thyme, bay leaf, peppercorns, and oil.

3. Transfer to a roasting pan and bake for 40 to 45 minutes, or until the potatoes are cooked through. Remove the potatoes from the roasting pan and refrigerate until cool.

4. In a medium bowl, whisk the mayonnaise, eggs, onion, celery, mustard, parsley, and tarragon.

5. Cut the chilled potatoes into ¼-inch-thick rounds and transfer to a large bowl. Toss with the mayonnaise dressing and refrigerate for at least 2 hours. Let the potato salad come to room temperature before serving.

3
GRAINS and PASTA and OTHER GOOD THINGS

AHH, THE GREATNESS THAT IS starch, gluten, and carbs! I swear, the more the "experts" tell ya to avoid 'em, the more you want 'em. Since I started my journey to a healthier lifestyle, I can't eat nearly as much of these tantalizing foods as I used to, but that doesn't mean I don't still love to cook and serve fettuccini, risotto, and quinoa.

What I find most fascinating about these recipes is that there is greater focus on craftsmanship than artistry. There's real science behind the cooking process, so you have less wiggle room. Think about it. There's a reason pasta and grain cookery hasn't really changed in the last three thousand years. There's a right way to do it. This doesn't mean you can't put your own twist on these recipes, but don't say I didn't warn you.

Quinoa with Apples and Cashews

{**SERVES 6**}

ALL HAIL QUINOA, the superfood! Do you know how to say it? I didn't for the longest time, and for the first five years of my culinary life I said "kwin-oh-ah," and nobody corrected me. My guess is either they didn't know how to say it themselves, or they didn't wanna make me feel bad. (Or they wanted me to look stupid!) Anyhow, I now know to say "KEEN-wah" and also absolutely adore this ancient grain. I like it in a salad with kale and a simple lemon vinaigrette, or, as here, with fresh herbs and some apples and cashews tossed in for texture and sweetness. To make this a little more robust, add some farro, wild rice, or amaranth (another ancient food).

PREP TIME: **ABOUT 15 MINUTES, PLUS STANDING**
COOKING TIME: **ABOUT 20 MINUTES**

1 teaspoon olive oil

1½ cups red quinoa

4 apples (such as Honeycrisp, Empire, or Mutsu), unpeeled, cored, and diced

3 tablespoons apple juice

2 tablespoons fresh lemon juice

2 teaspoons apple cider vinegar

½ cup chopped toasted cashews

1 shallot, minced

1 tablespoon coarsely chopped flat-leaf parsley

1 tablespoon minced fresh chives

1½ teaspoons chopped fresh tarragon

3 tablespoons extra-virgin olive oil

Salt and freshly ground black pepper

1. In a large saucepan, heat the olive oil over medium-high heat. When hot, toast the quinoa for about 5 minutes, stirring continuously. Add 3 cups of hot water and bring to a simmer. Reduce the heat to low, cover the pot, and simmer for about 15 minutes, until all the liquid has been absorbed. Remove from the heat and let the quinoa stand for about 5 minutes.

2. Fluff the quinoa with a fork and add the apples, apple juice, lemon juice, and vinegar. Set aside for about 15 minutes to give the flavors time to develop.

3. Add the cashews, shallot, parsley, chives, and tarragon and toss to mix. Add the extra-virgin olive oil and season with salt and pepper.

4. Serve warm or let the quinoa cool to room temperature before serving.

Farro with Dried Fruits and Nuts

Quinoa with Apples and Cashews

Artisan Grit Cakes

Cheddar Cheese Risotto {SERVES 4 TO 6}

AWW, YEAH. THIS IS A FUN rice dish that was inspired by a road trip through Wisconsin. We all know and love classic risotto, made with Parmesan cheese, and so I thought, "Hey! Let's celebrate the Midwest by using Wisconsin cheddar instead." It was a good idea. I dress it up a little with bacon "powder," some glazed onions, and apples and chives. The bacon and the onions require some advance planning, but once you get them out of the way, the risotto is easy.

PREP TIME: **ABOUT 35 MINUTES, PLUS DRYING AND RESTING**
COOKING TIME: **ABOUT 1 HOUR**

BACON POWDER

4 slices thick-cut bacon, chopped into small pieces

APPLE GARNISH

2 Gala or similar firm, sweet apples, peeled, cored, and julienned (reserve the apple peelings)

2 tablespoons fresh lemon juice

1 cup grenadine

½ cup apple cider vinegar

¼ cup packed brown sugar

GLAZED ONIONS

2 tablespoons unsalted butter

2 cups peeled pearl onions

3 tablespoons hard cider

RISOTTO

2 tablespoons olive oil

1 cup minced onions

2 cups arborio rice

3 cups dry white wine

4 ounces Wisconsin cheddar cheese, shredded (about 1 cup)

2 ounces mascarpone (about ¼ cup)

Salt and coarsely ground black pepper

1 bunch chives, finely chopped, for garnish

1. For the bacon powder, in a small frying pan, slowly cook the bacon over medium-low heat. Spoon the fat off and discard as the bacon cooks. When the bacon browns, use a slotted spoon to transfer the bacon to a fine-mesh sieve or chinois to drain a little more. Spread the bacon pieces on paper towels and allow the bacon to air-dry for 2 to 3 hours.

2. Grind the bacon pieces in a spice or coffee grinder. Spread the powder on paper towels and let it air-dry for at least 6 hours. The powder can be made up to 2 days ahead and stored in a lidded container at room temperature until ready to use.

3. For the apple garnish, in a small bowl, toss the julienned apples with the lemon juice. Add some cold water to cover the apples and set aside for up to 4 hours.

4. In a small saucepan, combine the grenadine, vinegar, and brown sugar with the reserved apple peelings. Bring to a boil over medium-high heat, reduce the heat, and simmer for about 5 minutes, or until the syrup has reduced to the consistency of honey. Transfer the syrup to a blender and puree until smooth. Set aside until needed.

5. For the glazed onions, in a large sauté pan, melt the butter over medium-high heat. When hot, cook the pearl onions for about 15 minutes, or until browned and tender.

6. Add the hard cider, reduce the heat to medium, and cook for about 30 minutes longer, or until the onions are cooked through. Lift the onions from the cooking liquid and set aside, covered to keep warm, until needed.

7. For the risotto, in a large saucepan, bring about 3 cups of water to a boil. Reduce the heat so that it's barely simmering but is very hot.

8. In a large, deep pot, heat the oil over medium-high heat and sauté the minced onions for 4 to 5 minutes, or until translucent. Add the rice and stir with a wooden spoon to mix well with the onions. Cook for 5 minutes longer.

9. Reduce the heat to medium-low and add 1 cup of the wine, stirring the rice and wine continuously with the wooden spoon. When the first cup of wine has been absorbed by the rice, add another cup. Stir the rice and wine, and add the final cup of wine when the rice has absorbed the second cup. As you stir, the rice will release its natural starches, which help absorb the liquid.

10. Begin adding the hot water in ¼-cup increments, stirring all the while. When you have added about 1 cup of the hot water, start tasting the rice and when it's al dente and has a little toothiness, stop adding water. This entire process should take about 20 minutes. Keep the hot water on the stove.

11. Add the cheddar and mascarpone to the hot risotto. Stir to allow the cheese to melt into the rice. Gently stir in the glazed onions. Season with salt and pepper. (Make sure you use enough pepper, which helps cut through the flavors of the dish.)

12. Divide the risotto among four to six serving plates or shallow bowls. Drain and pat dry the julienned apples and garnish each serving with the apples, chives, and bacon powder. Spoon the pureed apple peelings around the outside of the dish.

Coconut Rice {SERVES 6}

I LIVED IN HAWAII and the Philippines for a number of years, so it's safe to say I am something of a rice aficionado. Here's a simple dish that can be used as a side for fish or chicken, and it also makes very good fried rice. It goes well with pineapple, mango, chiles, cilantro, or basil . . . you name it. But stay away from heavier ingredients such as cream and butter to let the rich coconut shine through.

PREP TIME: **ABOUT 5 MINUTES, PLUS RESTING**
COOKING TIME: **ABOUT 25 MINUTES**

2 cups jasmine or basmati rice

1½ cups unsweetened coconut milk

1 teaspoon salt

2 to 3 tablespoons chopped cilantro

1 tablespoon grated lime zest

1. Put the rice in a colander and rinse under cold running water until the water runs clear.

2. Put the rice in a large saucepan with the coconut milk, salt, and 1½ cups of water. Bring to a boil. As soon as the liquid boils, reduce the heat to low, tightly cover the pan, and cook for about 18 minutes, or until all the liquid has been absorbed.

3. Remove the saucepan from the heat and let stand, covered, for 10 minutes. Remove the lid and fluff the rice with a fork. Fold in the cilantro and lime zest.

Chinese Forbidden Fried Rice {SERVES 6}

THIS BEAUTIFUL PURPLY-BLACK RICE was originally grown expressly for Chinese royalty. No one else could eat it, hence the name. Or at least that's what we chefs have been told, which means it could be a load of BS. But I like the story so I'm stickin' to it. And I've lived in the Philippines and Hawaii, so I have a firm grasp of the mysteries of fried rice. Hell, I should; I've probably consumed more than a hundred pounds of the stuff over the past three decades! As soon as I saw the dark hue of forbidden rice, I knew it would be supercool as the main component of fried rice. It goes especially well with crispy chicken or duck, but you could also serve it alongside grilled fish—I suggest mahi or grouper.

PREP TIME: ABOUT 10 MINUTES, PLUS CHILLING
COOKING TIME: 20 TO 25 MINUTES

1 cup black rice (also called forbidden rice)

½ teaspoon salt

3 tablespoons sesame oil

3 garlic cloves, minced

1 small carrot, peeled and diced

½ cup diced ham

1 bunch scallions, white and light green parts, chopped separately

1 tablespoon minced fresh ginger

1 teaspoon sambal chili sauce

3 large eggs, lightly beaten

1 cup frozen peas, thawed

3 tablespoons soy sauce

2 to 3 tablespoons chopped cilantro, for garnish

1. Put the rice in a large pot and add 3 cups of water and the salt. Bring to a boil and immediately reduce the heat to low, cover, and cook for 18 to 20 minutes, or until the liquid has been absorbed. Remove the pot from the heat and let stand, covered, for about 10 minutes. Fluff the rice with a fork.

2. Cover the rice and refrigerate for at least 2 hours, or until chilled.

3. In a wok or skillet, heat the sesame oil over medium-high heat. When hot, sauté the garlic, carrot, ham, white parts of the scallions, ginger, and chili sauce for 2 to 3 minutes, or until the carrot and scallions start to soften.

4. Add the eggs and stir vigorously until the eggs are half cooked. Add the peas and cooked rice and stir-fry until the rice heats through and begins to turn crispy. Stir in the soy sauce and 1 tablespoon of water. Cook for about 3 minutes longer, stirring, until the liquid has been absorbed.

5. Transfer the fried rice to a platter and garnish with the green parts of the scallions and the cilantro.

Farro with Dried Fruits and Nuts {SERVES 6}

NOW THAT I AM EATING more healthfully, I am a firm believer in farro, which is made from wheat and closely resembles spelt. It's rich and nutty, with an amazing texture that has the perfect amount of "chew." Plus, it's good for you! You can get all crazy and cook it in a way that's similar to risotto, or ease up a little and serve it as a cold grain salad. I like this in the summer, and then once the leaves start to change and autumn comes knocking on the door, I stuff the fruity grain salad in acorn squash to make a substantial meal.

PREP TIME: **ABOUT 10 MINUTES, PLUS RESTING**
COOKING TIME: **ABOUT 55 MINUTES**

½ cup olive oil

1 small yellow or white onion, minced

3 garlic cloves, thinly sliced

2 fresh bay leaves

Pinch of red pepper flakes

2 cups farro

8 cups chicken or vegetable stock, preferably homemade

Salt and freshly cracked black pepper

1 small red onion, diced

½ cup diced dried apricots

½ cup golden raisins

½ cup diced dried apples

½ cup marcona almonds

¼ cup toasted and crushed pistachios

1 teaspoon ground sumac

1 teaspoon piment d'Espelette, cayenne pepper, or hot paprika

Grated zest and juice of 1 lemon

1 teaspoon aged sherry vinegar

1 bunch flat-leaf parsley, coarsely chopped

2 tablespoons extra-virgin olive oil

1. In a Dutch oven or similar pot, heat a film of the olive oil over medium-high heat. When hot, cook the onion, garlic, bay leaves, and red pepper flakes for 5 to 6 minutes or until the onion is translucent and aromatic.

2. Add the farro and cook, stirring, for 2 to 3 minutes to toast the grain. Add the stock, stir, cover, and cook over low heat for about 45 minutes, until all the liquid has been absorbed and the farro is tender. Remove and discard the bay leaves.

3. Season with salt and pepper and stir in the remaining olive oil. The farro should taste nutty and have a little bite, but should not be starchy. Transfer the farro to a shallow bowl and let it cool.

4. When the farro is at room temperature, fold in the red onion, apricots, raisins, apples, almonds, and pistachios. Season with the sumac, piment d'Espelette, lemon zest, and vinegar. Mix well and season with salt. Let the farro sit at room temperature for about 30 minutes.

5. Gently stir the parsley, lemon juice, and extra-virgin olive oil into the farro and serve.

Artisan Grit Cakes {SERVES 6}

"ARTISAN" IS ONE OF THOSE WORDS that has been hijacked by "the man," aka corporations that have nothing to do with anything "artisan." In this recipe, the grits are artisan. Rather than using mass-produced, machine-ground hominy (dried, boiled, and cracked corn), these grit cakes are made with hand-ground hominy from an old mill in South Carolina. It makes a difference, and while you can buy them from other companies, I am particularly attached to Three Sisters Garden. Artisan grits take longer to cook, but the end result is well worth the extra time.

PREP TIME: **20 TO 25 MINUTES**
COOKING TIME: **ABOUT 55 MINUTES**

2 ears corn

Olive oil, for rubbing

8 tablespoons (1 stick) unsalted butter

1 small onion, diced

2 garlic cloves, sliced

4 cups whole milk

Kosher salt

1 cup artisan grits

1 cup Wondra flour

¼ cup canola oil

1. Prepare a charcoal or gas grill so that the coals or heating elements are medium-hot.

2. Remove the outer leaves from the corn husks, leaving most of the husk in place. Pull the husk back to expose the ear of corn, but do not remove it. Remove and discard the silk. Rub the corn with a little oil and replace the husks. If necessary, tie with kitchen twine.

3. Grill the corn for about 15 minutes, turning the ears every few minutes to encourage even grilling. When the outside of the husks starts to char and you can see outlines of the corn kernels through them, the corn is done. Lift the corn from the grill and when they're cool enough to handle, remove the husks and then slice the corn from the cobs. You should have about 1 cup of corn kernels.

4. In a deep pot, melt the butter over medium-high heat. When hot, cook the onion and garlic, stirring, for 5 to 6 minutes, or until the onion is translucent and aromatic.

5. Stir in the milk and 2 tablespoons of salt and bring to a simmer. Slowly whisk in the grits, making sure they don't clump. When the mixture is smooth, reduce the heat to low and cook gently for about 30 minutes, stirring often, until the grits are thick and creamy.

6. Line a baking sheet with parchment paper. Fold the grilled corn into the grits and then spread the mixture evenly onto the lined baking sheet and let it cool.

7. Using a knife or cookie cutter, cut the cooled grits into shapes. Dust them with the Wondra.

8. In a sauté pan, heat the canola oil over medium-high heat. When hot, sauté the grit cakes for 2 to 3 minutes on each side until golden brown. Season with salt and serve.

Fettuccini with Clams and Fennel Pesto {SERVES 6}

TASTING OF LICORICE-LIKE ANISE, fennel is something you either love or hate—much like cilantro. I love it so much that I tried to convince my wife, Allie, to name a baby girl "Fennel," should we have one. Three boys later, Allie has stopped worrying. The fronds can be used as an ingredient, too, and here I switch them out for the usual basil to make a pesto, which pairs perfectly with clams and fettuccini. Here's another tip: use a splash of Pernod when steaming the clams for a more concentrated anise flavor. And to really lift this to new levels, add the fennel pollen. It's probably not in your spice rack, but seek it out to use here. You won't be sorry.

PREP TIME: **ABOUT 10 MINUTES**
COOKING TIME: **12 TO 15 MINUTES**

PESTO

1 garlic clove, coarsely chopped

1 tablespoon pine nuts, toasted

1 teaspoon fennel seeds

¼ cup olive oil

Salt

Fronds from 1 fennel bulb, chopped

½ cup chopped flat-leaf parsley

Grated zest of 1 lemon

CLAMS AND PASTA

6 tablespoons olive oil

2 garlic cloves, thinly sliced

1 small fennel bulb, stems and bulb diced

1 shallot, minced

½ teaspoon red pepper flakes

1 fresh or dried bay leaf

30 fresh Manila or littleneck clams

1 cup white wine

¼ cup Pernod

1 cup heavy cream

1 pound fresh fettuccini

Juice of 1 lemon

Salt

1 cup toasted bread crumbs

1 teaspoon fennel pollen (optional)

1. For the pesto, put the garlic, pine nuts, and fennel seeds in a mortar and, using the pestle, grind the ingredients with a drizzle of oil until it becomes a homogenized paste. Add a little more oil, if needed. Season with salt.

2. Add the fennel fronds and parsley and grind until the pesto is bright green and the consistency of a fine paste. Stir in the lemon zest and season with salt. Set aside.

3. For the clams and pasta, in a deep pot, heat the oil over medium heat. When it shimmers, cook the garlic, diced fennel, shallot, red pepper flakes, and bay leaf for 2 to 3 minutes, or until the garlic turns golden and the mixture is aromatic.

4. Add the clams, wine, and Pernod to the pot. Add 1 cup of water, cover the pot, and raise the heat to medium-high. Let the clams steam for 3 to 4 minutes, or until they open. Gently remove the clams from the pot with tongs or a slotted spoon as they open and set aside, covered, to keep warm. (Discard any clams that do not open.) Strain the cooking liquid through a fine-mesh sieve or double layer of cheesecloth to remove any grit. Return the strained liquid and aromatic ingredients to the pot.

5. Stir the pesto and cream into the mixture in the pot and simmer for 2 to 3 minutes, or until the sauce comes together. Remove and discard the bay leaf.

6. Meanwhile, bring a large pot of salted water to a boil. Cook the pasta for 2 to 3 minutes. Drain, reserving 1 cup of the pasta cooking water. Toss the pasta with the pesto-cream sauce and add the reserved pasta cooking water. Add the clams and toss over low heat until everything is warm.

7. Stir in the lemon juice and season with salt. Sprinkle the pasta with the bread crumbs and the fennel pollen, if using. Serve right away.

Arancini with Roasted Garlic Aioli

{SERVES 6 TO 8; MAKES 20}

WHAT'S ARANCINI? YOU MIGHT ASK. Answer: small, bite-size balls of fried risotto, that's what. In other words, crunchy, creamy, cheesy goodness. They're so tasty, it's worth making risotto so you can fry it, but these are also a swell way to use up leftover risotto. (And let's face it, risotto the next day is pretty nasty, much like mac 'n' cheese is.) What makes these arancini stand out is the flavor punch of roasted garlic aioli.

PREP TIME: **ABOUT 25 MINUTES, PLUS CHILLING**
COOKING TIME: **ABOUT 35 MINUTES**

AIOLI

Pulp from 1 head roasted garlic (see page 86)

3 large egg yolks

1 teaspoon Dijon mustard

½ teaspoon champagne vinegar

½ cup extra-virgin olive oil

¼ cup grapeseed oil

1 teaspoon fresh lemon juice

1 teaspoon salt

ARANCINI

¼ cup olive oil

1 small onion, diced

1 fresh bay leaf

2 cups carnaroli or arborio rice

½ cup white wine or dry sherry

6 cups hot chicken or vegetable stock

3 ounces Parmesan cheese, shaved

Salt

2 tablespoons minced flat-leaf parsley

4 ounces aged sheep's-milk cheese or mozzarella or Fontina cheese, cut into small cubes

3 cups all-purpose flour

4 large eggs, whisked

3 cups panko bread crumbs

Freshly ground black pepper

Vegetable oil, for frying

1. For the aioli, put the garlic pulp, egg yolks, mustard, and vinegar in the bowl of a food processor fitted with the metal blade and pulse until smooth. With the motor running, add the extra-virgin olive oil and grapeseed oil in a slow, steady stream through the feed tube. When the mayonnaise is emulsified, transfer it to a bowl and season with lemon juice and salt. Taste and adjust the seasoning, if necessary. Use right away or refrigerate the aioli until needed.

2. For the arancini, in a heavy pot, heat a film of olive oil over medium-high heat. When hot, add the onion and bay leaf and cook for 2 to 3 minutes, until the onion softens. Add the rice and stir for a few minutes until it smells nutty (this is called "parching the rice"). Add the wine and cook, stirring, until the wine has been absorbed.

3. Slowly add ladles of the hot stock, stirring after each addition until the liquid has been absorbed before adding the next. This will take about 20 minutes and at the end, the risotto will be creamy and all the liquid will have been absorbed.

4. Fold the Parmesan into the risotto and season with salt. When the cheese is melted and incorporated, fold in the parsley.

5. Spoon the risotto onto a parchment paper–lined baking sheet and let it cool slightly. Refrigerate for several hours, or until completely cool.

6. Using an ice-cream scoop, scoop the risotto into 20 portions. With dampened palms, gently roll the portions into balls. Insert a piece of sheep's-milk cheese into the center of each rice ball.

7. Arrange three shallow bowls on a work surface, the first for the flour, the next for the beaten egg, and the last for the bread crumbs. Season the flour with salt and pepper.

8. Roll each rice ball first in the flour, then in the egg, and finally in the bread crumbs.

9. Return the rice balls to the baking sheet and refrigerate for at least 30 minutes and up to several hours.

10. Pour vegetable oil into a deep, heavy pot to a depth of about 3 inches, or use a deep-fat fryer. Heat the oil over medium-high heat to a temperature of 325°F. Use a deep-fry thermometer to test the temperature.

11. Fry the rice balls for about 5 minutes, or until golden brown. Do not crowd the pan while frying; fry only a few arancini at a time. Lift them from the oil with a slotted spoon and drain on paper towels.

12. Serve the arancini hot with the aioli for dipping.

How to Roast Garlic To roast a head of garlic, slice off the top and bottom of the bulb. Peel off the excess papery skin but leave the bulb intact. Set the garlic bulb on a piece of aluminum foil and drizzle olive oil over it. Use enough oil to fill the visible nooks and crannies. Season lightly with salt and pepper. Wrap the head of garlic tightly in the foil. Roast in a preheated 400°F oven for 30 to 35 minutes, or until the garlic cloves are soft.

Let the head of garlic cool and when cool enough to handle, pull away most of the skin and then squeeze the roasted cloves from the skins. Use the roasted garlic as needed. And you'll "need" it pretty often once you get a taste for it.

Ricotta Gnudi with Crispy Sage and Hazelnuts {SERVES 6}

GNUDI ARE GNOCCHI'S BIG BROTHER. The ricotta cheese makes this especially subtle and creamy, almost to the point of melt-in-your-mouth-ness. Like so many other pasta dishes, this tastes awesome with crispy sage and hazelnuts. I know the pairing is super predictable, but seriously, make it yourself and savor the flavors. Maybe you can even make it better!

PREP TIME: **ABOUT 20 MINUTES, PLUS DRAINING AND CHILLING**
COOKING TIME: **10 TO 15 MINUTES**

1 pound sheep's-milk ricotta cheese or other high-quality ricotta (about 2 cups)

1 large egg, plus 1 large egg yolk

2 ounces Parmesan cheese, grated (about ½ cup)

1 ounce Pecorino Sardo cheese, finely chopped or grated, about ¼ cup (see Note)

1 tablespoon minced fresh chives

1 teaspoon freshly grated nutmeg

½ teaspoon freshly ground white pepper

Salt

¼ cup fresh bread crumbs

¾ cup all-purpose flour

Semolina flour, for coating and dusting

8 tablespoons (1 stick) unsalted butter

10 fresh sage leaves

¼ cup chopped toasted hazelnuts

1 teaspoon date vinegar (optional)

2 ounces aged sheep's- or goat's-milk cheese, shaved (I like Evalon from LaClare Farms in Wisconsin or a good asiago)

1 tablespoon hazelnut oil

1. Put the ricotta in a fine-mesh sieve set over a pot or bowl and refrigerate overnight to give it time to drain. (You can use cheesecloth to drain the cheese, as well.)

2. In a large bowl, whisk the egg, egg yolk, Parmesan, pecorino, chives, nutmeg, pepper, and about 1 teaspoon of salt. Fold in the bread crumbs and ricotta. Sprinkle the batter with the all-purpose flour and gently fold it in. Cover the bowl with plastic wrap or a dish towel and refrigerate for at least 1 hour.

3. Line a baking sheet with parchment paper and sprinkle it with semolina.

4. With floured hands, form the chilled dough into 1-inch cylinders. Spread semolina in a shallow bowl and roll the gnudi in the semolina. As each one is coated, set it on the baking sheet.

5. Bring a large pot filled about halfway with liberally salted water to a boil. Drop the gnudi into the boiling water and cook for 7 to 8 minutes, or until they bob to the surface and are tender. Work in batches if necessary to avoid crowding the pot.

6. Lift the gnudi gently from the boiling water with a slotted spoon. Dab dry on paper towels and then transfer to a serving bowl.

7. Meanwhile, in a skillet, melt the butter over medium-high heat. When bubbling, fry the sage leaves in the butter for 2 to 3 minutes, or until crispy. Lift the sage leaves from the skillet and set aside. Salt them lightly.

8. Add the hazelnuts and vinegar, if using, to the butter and cook for about 30 seconds, until heated through. Pour the nuts over the gnudi and top with the sage, shaved cheese, and a drizzle of oil.

NOTE: Pecorino Sardo cheese is a firm cheese from Italy that is also known as fiore sardo and Pecorino Toscano. It's not widely available in the United States; use Pecorino Romano or duro as a good substitute.

Season with Salt

I don't usually specify the kind of salt you should use in my recipes. Some folks call for sea salt or kosher salt, and while I like and use both of these, table salt—the stuff that comes in those cylindrical canisters—works just fine. But be aware that it's treated with iodine, a necessary nutrient, so it may have a slight chemical flavor.

More important, if ya ask me, is how you use salt. When I say to season with salt, do so at the end of cooking. While I am a fan of seasoning and tasting as you go along, sometimes you run the risk of oversalting, so be cool; hold back and adjust accordingly.

When you make vinaigrettes, dissolve the salt in the vinegar before you mix it with the olive oil; when you cook pasta, salt the water once it comes to a boil; a pinch of salt perks up sweet flavors, just as it perks up savory ones.

Fancy salts add great flavor to lots of dishes, although rarely are they used to season food as you cook. Instead, they are lovely finishing-school grads, poised to add grace to dishes throughout the meal. These beauts include the beloved fleur de sel, as well as Maldon, Hawaiian red, and Cyprus black. Their grain often is larger than ordinary salt.

Pumpkin Ravioli with Pears and Pomegranate Seeds {SERVES 6}

WHO DOESN'T LOVE CLASSIC pumpkin ravioli? It's ubiquitous in autumn for the best reason of all: It's damn tasty! To make it a li'l different, I decided to use the lesser known but equally delicious red kuri squash. Pomegranates and pears pull the dish together with their innate sweetness and acidity, and the pomegranate seeds also provide some welcome crunch. Remember: You can use trusty butternut, acorn, or pumpkin squash instead, but seek out red kuri to prove that you can use esoteric ingredients that no one's even heard of!

PREP TIME: **ABOUT 1 HOUR 20 MINUTES, PLUS CHILLING**
COOKING TIME: **35 TO 40 MINUTES**

PASTA DOUGH

- 1¾ cups all-purpose flour, plus more for dusting
- 6 large egg yolks
- 1 large egg
- 1 tablespoon milk
- 1 tablespoon olive oil

PUMPKIN FILLING

- 3 pounds red kuri squash (about 2), peeled and halved (see Note)
- 8 ounces (2 sticks) unsalted butter
- 1½ cups pure maple syrup
- Salt
- 4 fresh sage leaves
- 4 cinnamon sticks

- 8 ounces mascarpone cheese (about 1 cup)
- Juice of 1 lemon
- 2 large eggs, lightly beaten, for egg wash

PEARS AND POMEGRANATE SEEDS

- 2 Bosc pears, peeled, cored, and diced
- 1 small kohlrabi, peeled and diced
- ½ cup pomegranate seeds
- 1 shallot, minced
- 2 fresh sage leaves, minced
- 1 tablespoon minced fresh thyme
- 1 tablespoon olive oil
- 1 teaspoon fresh lemon juice
- 1 tablespoon toasted pumpkin seeds, coarsely chopped (see Note)
- Salt and freshly ground black pepper

1. For the pasta dough, put the flour in a large bowl and make a well in the center. Add the egg yolks, egg, milk, and oil to the well. Pull the flour from around the sides of the well into the wet ingredients, gently breaking up the eggs with your fingers. Work around the circle formed by the flour and the well until the dough resembles a sticky paste.

2. Turn the dough out onto a lightly floured surface and knead gently until the dough is smooth and bounces back slightly when you press it with your finger. Form the dough into a ball and wrap well with plastic wrap. Refrigerate for at least 45 minutes, or longer if it fits with your schedule.

3. For the pumpkin filling, preheat the oven to 400°F. Line a baking sheet with aluminum foil.

4. Put the squash on the baking sheet, cut side up. Dot with the butter and drizzle with the maple syrup. Season with salt. Put the sage leaves and cinnamon sticks on top of the squash. Bake for 30 to 35 minutes, or until tender.

5. Let the squash cool. Transfer the cooled squash only (not the cinnamon or sage) to the bowl of a food processor fitted with the metal blade and process until smooth. Add the mascarpone and lemon juice. Pulse to mix and season with salt, if needed.

6. Unwrap the chilled dough and set it on a lightly floured surface. Divide the dough into 6 pieces and using a lightly floured rolling pin, roll each piece into a 4 x 19-inch rectangle.

7. Put 9 rounded teaspoons of filling just off center down the rectangle, leaving about 1 inch between each one.

8. Brush a little egg wash along both sides of the dough and fold the dough over the filling. With your fingers, press the edges of the dough around the filling. Using a pizza cutter, cut out the ravioli and transfer to a floured baking sheet or platter. Continue to make ravioli with the remaining dough and filling. Refrigerate for at least 30 minutes to let them set up.

9. Bring a large pot of salted water to a boil. Drop the ravioli in the boiling water and cook for 3 to 5 minutes, or until they bob to the surface. Remove one of the ravioli and pop it in your mouth. Take a bite to make sure it's hot in the center. If so, the ravioli are good to go. If not, cook for another minute or so until the centers are hot. Drain the ravioli.

10. For the pears and pomegranate seeds, in a large bowl, toss the pears, kohlrabi, pomegranate seeds, shallot, sage, thyme, oil, and lemon juice. Add the pumpkin seeds and stir well. Season with salt and pepper.

11. Spoon the pears and pomegranate seeds over the ravioli and serve right away.

NOTE: Red kuri squash is a winter squash that resembles a small pumpkin. Its flesh is orange with a somewhat nutty, somewhat sweet flavor. You can substitute butternut or hubbard squash for red kuri.

To toast pumpkin seeds, spread the seeds in a dry skillet and cook over medium-high heat, shaking the pan, for 3 to 4 minutes, or until the seeds are lightly browned and aromatic. You can also buy toasted pumpkin seeds, sometimes called pepitas.

Potato Gnocchi with Shaved Pecorino and Brown Butter {SERVES 6}

THIS IS ONE OF THOSE CROWD-PLEASING dishes chefs put on the menu and then stand back and wait for the orders to pour in. It's a no-brainer, the restaurant equivalent of shooting fish in a barrel (which, while easy, doesn't sound like very much fun). You can keep this vegetarian or add some duck confit, roast chicken, or pulled pork. I'd stay away from anything "steak-y" that might make this difficult to eat. Roasted veggies like carrots or squash would go well with this, too.

A quick explanation about why I cook the spuds on a bed of salt: Salt being salt, it pulls the moisture from the potatoes as they cook. This results in a starchier, drier potato, which gives the potato-based dough better texture. Otherwise, you'd have to add tons of flour, which would make these more of a dumpling than the lighter gnocchi I'm after.

PREP TIME: 25 TO 30 MINUTES
COOKING TIME: 38 TO 40 MINUTES

2 cups kosher salt, plus more for seasoning

4 large Yukon Gold potatoes

2 large eggs

4 ounces Parmesan cheese, shaved (about 1 cup)

½ cup ricotta cheese

2½ cups all-purpose flour, plus more as needed

4 tablespoons (½ stick) unsalted butter

1 teaspoon fresh lemon juice

Freshly cracked black pepper

4 ounces pecorino duro cheese or another high-quality pecorino, shaved (about 1 cup)

1 or 2 teaspoons minced fresh chives

1. Preheat the oven to 400°F.

2. Spread the salt over the bottom of a small, shallow baking pan. Poke the potatoes with a fork or paring knife to make small holes. Set the potatoes on the salt and roast for about 30 minutes or until the skins begin to brown and the potatoes are cooked through. The cooking time depends on the size of the potatoes.

3. Remove the potatoes from the oven and score them to allow steam to escape. Cut the potatoes in half and scoop out the flesh. Use a ricer to rice the potatoes into a bowl.

4. Add the eggs, Parmesan, ricotta, and 1½ teaspoons of salt. Mix well and then gradually cut in 2½ cups of the flour. Gently knead the dough in the bowl until it forms a soft ball. Add a little more flour, if needed.

5. Turn the dough out onto a lightly floured work surface and pinch off small amounts. Roll each into a long snake about ½ inch in diameter. Cut the snakes into ¾-inch-long pieces. Gently pinch each gnocchi between your thumb and forefinger at each end. Set the gnocchi aside on the floured work surface.

6. Bring a large pot of lightly salted water to a boil. Drop the gnocchi into the boiling water in small batches and cook for about 4 minutes, or until the gnocchi float to the surface. Lift them from the water with a slotted spoon and set aside.

7. In a large skillet, heat the butter over medium-high heat and when melted and bubbling, stir in the lemon juice. Add the gnocchi and cook for 3 to 4 minutes, rolling until they brown and are coated with the butter. Season with salt and cracked black pepper.

8. Transfer the gnocchi to a serving bowl and top with the pecorino and chives. Serve right away.

4
CATCH o' the DAY

Grilled Swordfish with Charred
Pineapple and Mojo Verde

Atlantic Flounder with
Caramelized Cauliflower
and Raisin Chutney

Pan-Seared Snapper with
Purple Potatoes and Gingery
Baby Bok Choy

Roasted Black Cod with Melted
Leeks and Champagne Sauce

Wild Salmon with Swiss Chard
and Whipped Parsnips

Great Lakes Whitefish with
Buttermilk Ranch Tartar Sauce
and Fried Pickles

Pan-Seared Salmon with Napa
Cabbage Slaw and Whole-Grain
Mustard

Maple-Bourbon-Glazed Scallops
with Butternut Squash and
Swiss Chard

Crab Cakes with Charred
Corn Rémoulade

Lobster Schnitzel with Shaved
Asparagus and Citrus Vinaigrette

Lollapalooza Lobster Corn Dogs

Caribbean Shrimp Ceviche
with Mango Salsa

Steamed Mussels with
Mexican Chorizo and Cerveza

EVEN THOUGH I'VE BEEN to all fifty states and, as a military brat, grew up traveling the world, what always centers me and brings me "home" is the ocean. Actually, give me the seas, rivers, lakes, ponds, puddles . . . whatever, as long as it's wet and there's some seafood lurking beneath the surface.

My mom's family hails from southern Maryland, right on the Chesapeake Bay. My dad's folks are from Michigan, one of the most watery states, and so I grew up surrounded by people who loved fishing. How lucky is that!

I'll always remember the first time I reeled in a bluefish, the first time I went spearfishing (I scored a three-foot octopus!), the first time I bit into a soft-shell crab sandwich, and the first time my dad brought home a giant spiny lobster for my birthday. That was something to celebrate.

These are some of the fond memories I look back on when people ask how I first got into cooking. I don't know about you, but I frequently rely on memories for inspiration, be it for cooking, music, art, or acting. And no doubt about it, the emotional connection with childhood provides a great springboard for creativity.

Grilled Swordfish with Charred Pineapple and Mojo Verde {SERVES 6}

SWORDFISH REMINDS ME of living in Hawaii, where we ate fish pretty much all the time. Swordfish are as meaty and flavorful as they are beautiful, and when a fish is as dense as this one, I gravitate toward the grill. The flame-licked flesh takes on an Old World smokiness that simply explodes with flavor when served alongside coconut and pineapple, the tropical twosome.

PREP TIME: ABOUT 20 MINUTES, PLUS MARINATING
COOKING TIME: 15 TO 18 MINUTES

SWORDFISH

- 1 cup olive oil
- 4 garlic cloves, minced
- 4 sprigs fresh thyme
- 1 tablespoon minced fresh oregano
- 1 teaspoon ground sumac
- 1 teaspoon red pepper flakes
- Grated zest of 2 lemons
- Grated zest of 1 lime
- 2 pounds center-cut swordfish, cut into 6 equal steaks
- Salt and freshly ground black pepper
- 3 limes, halved

MOJO VERDE

- ½ white onion, diced
- 2 garlic cloves
- 1 serrano chile, seeded and diced
- ¼ teaspoon cumin seeds
- ¼ teaspoon coriander seeds
- 1 large bunch cilantro, coarsely chopped
- ½ cup olive oil
- 1 tablespoon sherry vinegar
- Salt

CHARRED PINEAPPLE

- 1 pineapple, peeled, cored, and cut lengthwise into planks
- 1 tablespoon piment d'Espelette, cayenne pepper, or hot paprika
- 1½ teaspoons cumin seeds
- Coconut Rice (page 75)

1. For the swordfish, put the oil, garlic, thyme, oregano, sumac, red pepper flakes, and lemon and lime zests in a large resealable plastic bag. Shake the bag to mix well.

2. Lightly season the swordfish on both sides with salt and black pepper. Put the fish in the bag and manipulate the steaks carefully so that they are coated with the marinade. Refrigerate the swordfish for about 2 hours, turning the bag several times during marinating.

3. For the mojo verde, in a cast-iron skillet, dry roast the onion, garlic cloves, and chile over medium-high heat for about 8 minutes, until the vegetables begin to caramelize. Add the cumin and coriander seeds and toast for about 30 seconds. Pour a splash of water into the pan to deglaze it and prevent the other ingredients from sticking.

4. Transfer the onion mixture to a blender and add the cilantro and 1 cup of water. Blend until smooth. With the motor running, slowly add the oil until emulsified. As the mixture comes together, add the oil a little more quickly and the vinegar. When smooth, season with salt. Cover and set aside until needed.

5. For the charred pineapple, rub the pineapple planks with piment d'Espelette and cumin.

6. Prepare a gas or charcoal grill so that the heating elements or coals are medium-hot. Lift the swordfish from the marinade and let the excess drip back into the bag. Season with a little more salt and black pepper and grill for 3 minutes on each side for medium to medium-well fish.

7. Put the pineapple planks on the grill and char for 2 to 3 minutes on each side.

8. Spoon some rice onto each of six serving plates and top each with a swordfish steak. Squeeze lime juice from the halved limes over the fish. Spoon some mojo verde on top and serve with the charred pineapple on the side.

Wild-Caught Fish for Dinner

The opposite of farm-raised fish is wild-caught fish. But fish labeled "wild-caught" is not necessarily the better choice. Sure, the fish swim in open lakes, rivers, and oceans before they're caught, but they aren't necessarily caught in a sustainable manner. They might be caught in drift nets, which damage the ocean by scooping up everything in their path. On the other hand, some wild-caught fish are line-caught, which is the best way to haul them from the briny deep.

Without a doubt, we're overfishing our oceans. Here in the United States, we have regulations that protect the oceans' stores, but there are plenty of countries that don't or won't enforce similar actions. Be mindful when eating fish and seafood. Try to buy fish that is caught in the United States and check out the lists of sustainable fish available online. They change all the time, and it's tough to keep up—but we owe it to future generations to try.

Atlantic Flounder with Caramelized Cauliflower and Raisin Chutney {SERVES 6}

A LONG TIME AGO in a kitchen far, far away, Chef Jean-Georges Vongerichten discovered the miraculous pairing of cauliflower, almonds, and raisins. He decided to serve this ambrosia alongside scallops. I've taken a page outta his book (aka straight-up lifted/stole it) and matched it with the humble flounder. When I was a kid, I fished for flounder with my grandpa and have always been excited by how you immediately know when you have one on the line. Unlike tuna or mackerel, a flounder doesn't swim away from you but tries to stay firmly anchored on the sandy bottom. This makes landing one feel like you're trying to raise the *Titanic* off the goddamn ocean floor!

PREP TIME: **ABOUT 15 MINUTES**
COOKING TIME: **18 TO 20 MINUTES**

CAULIFLOWER

- 2 tablespoons olive oil
- 6 tablespoons (¾ stick) unsalted butter
- 1 tablespoon mild curry powder
- ½ small white onion, thinly sliced
- 1 garlic clove, thinly sliced
- 3 cups cauliflower florets (about 10 ounces)
- 1 tablespoon fresh lemon juice
- Salt

FLOUNDER

- 6 skinless flounder fillets (about 5 ounces each)
- Salt
- Wondra flour, for coating
- 6 tablespoons vegetable oil
- 6 tablespoons (¾ stick) unsalted butter
- Juice of 1 lemon
- Raisin Chutney (recipe follows)

1. For the cauliflower, in a Dutch oven or similar casserole dish, heat the oil and butter over medium-high heat until the butter bubbles. Add the curry powder and toast for about 30 seconds, or until the aroma develops. Add the onion and garlic, reduce the heat to medium-low, and cook, stirring, for 5 to 6 minutes, or until the onion is soft and lightly caramelized.

2. Add the cauliflower florets to the pot and roll them in the butter mixture until coated. Cook for about 10 minutes longer, stirring the florets to encourage even cooking, until they soften and turn a rich golden color and start to caramelize a little. Season with lemon juice and salt.

3. For the flounder, using paper towels, pat the fish fillets dry. Liberally season both sides of the fillets with salt and then coat them on both sides with Wondra.

4. In a large sauté pan or skillet, heat the oil over high heat until it shimmers. Slide 3 fillets into the pan in a forward direction so as not to splash the oil. Cook for about 3 minutes, or until the edges of the fish begin to brown. Using a spatula, turn the fish fillets over and add half the butter and half the lemon juice to the pan. When the butter melts, baste the fish with it. Cook for about 30 seconds longer and then transfer the fish to a serving platter. Repeat with the remaining fillets.

5. Serve the fish with the cauliflower and pass the chutney on the side.

Raisin Chutney {MAKES ABOUT 2 CUPS}

PREP TIME: **ABOUT 10 MINUTES**
COOKING TIME: **ABOUT 10 MINUTES**

½ cup dark raisins	2 tablespoons rice wine vinegar
½ cup golden raisins	2 tablespoons chopped cilantro
¼ cup black currants	1 tablespoon chopped mint leaves
1 shallot, thinly sliced	1 teaspoon ground sumac
1 fresh or dried bay leaf	1 teaspoon piment d'Espelette, cayenne pepper, or hot paprika
2 cups white verjus (see page 48)	Grated zest and juice of 2 limes
3 tablespoons honey	2 teaspoons salt

1. In a large saucepan, mix the raisins, currants, shallot, bay leaf, verjus, honey, and vinegar. Bring to a simmer over medium heat and cook for about 10 minutes, or until the fruit absorbs all the liquid and the raisins are plump. What's important is that the liquid is absorbed. Remove and discard the bay leaf.

2. Fold in the cilantro, mint, sumac, and piment d'Espelette and remove from the heat. Stir in the lime zest and juice and the salt.

3. Let the chutney cool to room temperature and then cover and refrigerate for at least 5 hours before serving.

Brick Red Espelette Piment d'Espelette

is made by grinding chiles that grow in the Basque regions of France and Spain, and takes its name from a small French town. When ground, the chili powder is brick red, with a flavor that is slightly fruity and gentle with a nip of a bite. Because of this piquancy, piment d'Espelette can be used in place of cayenne or hot paprika—or vice versa.

Pan-Seared Snapper with Purple Potatoes and Gingery Baby Bok Choy

{SERVES 4}

SNAPPER AND GINGERY BOK CHOY love each other madly, particularly when the snapper is nice and crisp. Score the fish's skin a few times so it will crisp up.

PREP TIME: **10 TO 12 MINUTES**
COOKING TIME: **ABOUT 8 MINUTES**

½ teaspoon cardamom seeds, toasted and crushed

4 tablespoons (½ stick) unsalted butter

Salt and freshly ground black pepper

12 ounces small purple potatoes, peeled

2 tablespoons sesame oil

1 tablespoon fresh lime juice

1 tablespoon soy sauce or tamari

2 to 3 scallions, trimmed, white and light green parts sliced on an angle, plus more greens for garnish

1 teaspoon minced jalapeño

1½ teaspoons minced fresh ginger

4 baby bok choy, halved lengthwise

1½ pounds skin-on snapper fillet, cut into 4 pieces

2 tablespoons canola oil

1 teaspoon toasted black sesame seeds, for garnish

1. Mix the cardamom seeds with the butter. Season with salt and pepper and set aside.

2. Bring a large saucepan filled with lightly salted water to a boil. Reduce the heat to medium and when the water simmers, add the potatoes and cook for 15 to 20 minutes, or until the potatoes are tender. Drain, return to the pan, cover, and set aside to keep warm.

3. In a small bowl, whisk the sesame oil, lime juice, and soy sauce. Add the scallions, jalapeño, and ginger and stir to mix. Season with salt and pepper.

4. Bring another large saucepan filled with lightly salted water to a boil. Set a bowl filled with cold water and ice cubes near the stove. Boil the bok choy for 15 to 20 seconds and submerge in the ice water to cool. Drain the bok choy.

5. Heat a stovetop grill or heavy skillet until very hot. If using a skillet, pour a little oil into it and when hot, cook the bok choy for 15 to 20 seconds on each side, until tender. Set aside.

6. Coat the snapper with the cardamom butter and season lightly with salt and pepper. Heat a large skillet over medium-high heat. When hot, add the oil and heat until it shimmers. Cook the fish, skin side down, for about 6 minutes, or until the fish is tender.

7. Whisk the vinaigrette. In a large bowl, toss the bok choy with the vinaigrette to coat.

8. Divide the potatoes among four serving plates. Top them with the bok choy and put the fish on top of the bok choy. Drizzle the remaining vinaigrette over the fish. Garnish with the sesame seeds and scallion greens and serve.

Roasted Black Cod with Melted Leeks and Champagne Sauce {SERVES 6}

OH YEAH. TIME TO BREAK OUT the fancy pants and get down and crazy with the bubbly! Champagne pairs well with damn near anything and everything. The sweetness, acidity, and crisp effervescence cut through richness like Voltron's sword! The natural buttery richness of black cod (or sable), which hails from the Pacific Ocean, easily stands up to the sauce, and finally, the leeks bring some much needed earthiness to the dish to tie it all together.

PREP TIME: **ABOUT 20 MINUTES**
COOKING TIME: **40 TO 45 MINUTES**

CHAMPAGNE SAUCE

- 1 cup dry Champagne
- 1 tablespoon Champagne vinegar
- 1 shallot, minced
- 2 sprigs fresh tarragon
- 1 sprig fresh thyme
- 1 fresh or dried bay leaf
- 4 whole black peppercorns
- 1 cup heavy cream
- 8 tablespoons (1 stick) chilled unsalted butter, cubed
- Salt
- Lemon juice

MELTED LEEKS

- 4 large leeks, trimmed of green stems and roots
- 6 ounces (1½ sticks) unsalted butter
- 2 fresh or dried bay leaves
- Salt and freshly cracked black pepper

BLACK COD

- 6 tablespoons vegetable oil
- 6 pieces Pacific black cod, skin removed (about 5 ounces each)
- Salt and freshly ground black pepper
- 6 tablespoons (¾ stick) unsalted butter
- 4 sprigs fresh thyme
- 2 garlic cloves, unpeeled
- Juice of 1 lemon
- Fleur de sel

1. To make the Champagne sauce, in a large saucepan, mix the Champagne, vinegar, shallot, tarragon, thyme, bay leaf, and peppercorns. Bring to a boil over medium-high heat, immediately reduce the heat, and simmer for about 5 minutes, until the sauce has reduced by about two-thirds.

2. Add the heavy cream and bring to a simmer. Cook for 4 to 5 minutes, until the cream is reduced by half. Remove from the heat and slowly whisk in the cold butter piece by piece, waiting until each cube is incorporated and emulsified before adding the next.

3. Strain the sauce through a fine-mesh sieve or chinois. Season with salt and lemon juice. Cover and set aside to keep warm.

4. To make the melted leeks, split the white parts of the leeks lengthwise and rinse them under cold, running water to remove any sand or grit. Slice the leeks thinly and put them in a Dutch oven or similar pot. Add the butter and bay leaves and season lightly with salt. Heat over low heat, stirring gently. Let the leeks cook for about 20 minutes, or until the leeks are tender but not colored. Season with salt and pepper. Cover to keep warm.

5. To make the black cod, preheat the oven to 400°F.

6. Divide the oil between two large, oven-safe skillets and heat over medium-high heat. Liberally season the fish with salt and pepper and when the oil is hot, cook the fish, flesh side down, for about 30 seconds, or until you feel the fish relax when pressed gently with your hand or a spatula. Continue cooking for 2 minutes more.

7. Transfer the skillets to the oven and roast for 5 minutes. Return the skillets to the stovetop. Turn the fish over.

8. Divide the butter, thyme, and garlic between the two pans. When the butter melts, baste the fish with the butter, spooning the melted butter over the fish for about 1 minute.

9. Transfer the fish to a serving platter. Season with lemon juice and fleur de sel. Spoon a little sauce over the fish and pass the rest at the table. Serve the leeks alongside the fish.

Wild Salmon with Swiss Chard and Whipped Parsnips {SERVES 4}

LATE-HARVEST GREENS, LIKE SWISS CHARD, make it easier to deal with the short, dark days of late autumn. You can't wait for dinner when they're on the menu, and that's a good thing! This dish is happily comforting and if you want to try it with rainbow chard instead of Swiss, the colors just pop off the plate. And the parsnips are irresistible, a little peppery and smelling like vanilla—truly the badass sisters of carrots.

PREP TIME: ABOUT 15 MINUTES
COOKING TIME: ABOUT 1 HOUR

1 pound parsnips, peeled and chopped

4 cups whole milk

5 sprigs fresh thyme

8 ounces slab bacon, diced

1 onion, diced

1 bunch Swiss chard, trimmed and chopped (about 1 pound)

1 (750-ml) bottle merlot or similar red wine

4 skin-on salmon fillets (1½ pounds total)

8 tablespoons (1 stick) unsalted butter

1. In large saucepan, cover the parsnips with the milk. Add the thyme and bring the mixture to a brisk simmer over medium-high heat. Reduce the heat and simmer for about 20 minutes, or until the parsnips are tender. Working in batches, if necessary, puree the parsnip mixture in a blender. Strain through a fine-mesh sieve. Return the puree to the pan and cover to keep warm.

2. Cook the bacon in a skillet over medium-high heat to render the fat. When the bacon is crispy and the fat has rendered, add the onion and sauté for 5 to 6 minutes, or until translucent. Add the Swiss chard and cook for about 5 minutes or until tender, stirring to mix the chard with the bacon and onion. Set aside, covered, to keep warm.

3. In another saucepan, bring the wine to a rapid simmer and cook until it has reduced to a saucelike consistency and is thick enough to coat the back of a spoon. This will take about 10 minutes.

4. Preheat the oven to 350°F.

5. Score the skin side of each salmon fillet with three lengthwise slits. This will allow the fat to escape and make the skin especially crispy.

6. In a deep, oven-safe sauté pan, melt the butter over medium-high heat. When hot, sear the salmon, skin side down, for 3 minutes. Transfer to the oven and cook for about 7 minutes, or until the salmon is just cooked through.

7. Spoon parsnip puree in the center of each of four serving plates and top with the Swiss chard hash. Angle a salmon fillet, skin side up, on the hash and drizzle the wine reduction around the plate.

Great Lakes Whitefish with Buttermilk Ranch Tartar Sauce and Fried Pickles

{SERVES 6}

THIS IS ONE OF THE FIRST DISHES I put on the menu at my first restaurant, so it has a special place in my heart. It's a play on the British classic fish 'n' chips, Americanized with ranch tartar sauce and some fried pickle action. Since I live in Chicago, whitefish pretty much swim in my backyard, i.e., Lake Michigan. The closer something grows (or swims) to your kitchen, the fresher it will be. Shorter travel!

PREP TIME: **12 TO 15 MINUTES**
COOKING TIME: **ABOUT 5 MINUTES**

TARTAR SAUCE

- 1 cup mayonnaise
- ½ cup low-fat buttermilk
- ¼ cup rinsed and chopped cornichons
- 1 tablespoon fresh lemon juice
- 1 tablespoon chopped drained capers
- 1 tablespoon chopped fresh dill
- 1 tablespoon chopped fresh tarragon
- 1 tablespoon minced fresh chives
- 1 teaspoon Dijon mustard
- 1 teaspoon Worcestershire sauce
- 1 teaspoon hot sauce (I like Crystal hot sauce)
- 1 shallot, minced
- Salt

WHITEFISH

- Fine cornmeal, for coating
- 6 whitefish fillets (about 5 ounces each)
- Salt
- 2 tablespoons canola oil
- 1 tablespoon unsalted butter
- 1 lemon wedge
- Fried Pickles (recipe follows)

1. For the tartar sauce, in a small bowl, stir all the ingredients except the salt. Taste and season with salt.

2. For the whitefish, spread the cornmeal on a plate or in a shallow bowl. Pat the fish with paper towels and when dry, season with salt on both sides. Gently coat the fish on both sides with cornmeal.

3. In a large sauté pan or skillet, heat the oil over high heat until it shimmers. Slide the fish into the pan in a forward direction so as not to splash the oil. Cook for about 3 minutes, or until the edges of the fish begin to brown. Using a spatula, turn the fish over and add the butter to the pan. When the butter melts, baste the fish with it. Cook for about 30 seconds longer and then transfer the fish to a baking sheet or pan lined with paper towels. Squeeze the lemon wedge over the fish.

4. Serve the fish with the tartar sauce and fried pickles.

Fried Pickles {MAKES ABOUT 2 CUPS}

PREP TIME: **ABOUT 20 MINUTES**
COOKING TIME: **3 TO 6 MINUTES**

2 large egg whites

1½ cups all-purpose flour

1 large egg

½ cup white cornmeal

1 cup cornstarch

1 teaspoon sugar

1 teaspoon cayenne pepper

3 cups canola oil

2 cups sliced bread-and-butter pickles

Salt

1. In the bowl of a stand mixer fitted with the whisk attachment, beat the egg whites until light and fluffy.

2. In a medium bowl, gently whisk ½ cup of the flour with 1 cup of water. Add the egg and cornmeal and whisk until smooth. Fold the egg whites into the flour mixture and set aside.

3. In another mixing bowl, whisk the remaining 1 cup of flour, the cornstarch, sugar, and cayenne.

4. In a deep, heavy pot, heat the oil over high heat until it registers 350°F on a deep-fry thermometer.

5. Dip the pickles first in the egg mixture and then in the flour mixture, brushing off any excess.

6. Gently drop the pickles in the hot oil and fry for 3 minutes, or until the pickles are golden brown. Do not overcrowd the oil. Lift the pickles from the oil with a slotted spoon, drain on paper towels, and season with salt.

Pan-Seared Salmon with Napa Cabbage Slaw and Whole-Grain Mustard {SERVES 4}

I CHANGED THE WAY I eat when I lost a lot of weight a while ago, and this salmon dish embodies how I care for my health. I look for pure, bold flavors nowadays, choosing them over carbs and fat whenever I can. The napa cabbage slaw bolsters up the salmon and believe me, it's not hard to make. The grainy mustard sauce, drizzled over the salmon just before serving, also provides a big flavor punch. I like to cook the salmon in a grill pan. It makes nice-looking marks on the fish, but more important, it elevates the fish just enough so that it does not sit in the fat and gets enough heat to cook quickly and thoroughly.

PREP TIME: 18 TO 20 MINUTES
COOKING TIME: ABOUT 8 MINUTES

1 medium head napa cabbage, trimmed

1 red onion

1 Granny Smith apple

2 tablespoons extra-virgin olive oil

Juice of 1 lemon

1 tablespoon whole-grain mustard

1 teaspoon apple cider vinegar

4 salmon fillets (about 6 ounces each)

Salt and freshly ground black pepper

1 tablespoon olive oil

1 bunch fresh chives, minced, for garnish

1. Using a mandoline or very sharp knife, shave or slice the cabbage as thinly as possible. Transfer the cabbage to a mixing bowl.

2. Using a mandoline or very sharp knife, shave or slice the onion as thinly as possible. Transfer to the bowl with the cabbage.

3. Peel and core the apple and slice into matchsticks. As you work, submerge the apple slices in a bowl of ice water to keep them from browning.

4. Drain the apple slices and gently shake or pat dry. Add the apples to the bowl with the cabbage and onion and toss.

5. In a small bowl, whisk 1 tablespoon of the extra-virgin olive oil and the lemon juice. Drizzle over the slaw, tossing to mix. Use only enough dressing to coat the slaw lightly.

6. In another bowl, whisk the remaining 1 tablespoon extra-virgin olive oil with the mustard and vinegar and set aside.

7. Season the salmon on both sides with salt and pepper. In a grill pan or large sauté pan, heat the olive oil over medium-high heat. When hot, cook the salmon for 3 to 4 minutes on each side.

8. Divide the slaw among four plates and top each serving with the salmon. Garnish the salmon with chives. Drizzle the mustard vinaigrette over the salmon and serve.

Maple-Bourbon-Glazed Scallops with Butternut Squash and Swiss Chard

{SERVES 4}

LOOKING FOR A NOT-SO-OBVIOUS fall dish? This is it. I originally put these scallops on the menu at the Jackson House Inn and Restaurant in Woodstock, Vermont, my first executive chef position, and have kept them in my back pocket for fall menus ever since.

The flavors and textures come together here as clearly as a deep blue October sky over the Green Mountains: Butternut squash means autumn to most of us; maple syrup says "New England" and marries perfectly with bourbon. Finally, scallops—the not-so-obvious piece—just fit with their mild, salty flavor and pleasingly soft texture. As the mighty Atlantic is only one small state away from Vermont, I could not resist. At the restaurant, we use hand-harvested diver scallops. Your local fish purveyor may have these for sale, but if not, buy the freshest and best scallops you can find. Blot the scallops dry with paper towels to ensure they take on some nice color when seared.

PREP TIME: ABOUT 30 MINUTES
COOKING TIME: ABOUT 1 HOUR

Salt

1 cup steel-cut Irish oats

½ cup whole milk

8 tablespoons (1 stick) unsalted butter

Freshly cracked black pepper

2 cups cubed (1-inch cubes) peeled butternut squash (about 10 ounces)

4 tablespoons canola oil

2 sprigs fresh sage

2 sprigs fresh thyme

Freshly cracked black pepper

¾ cup chicken stock, preferably homemade

1 small bunch rainbow chard (about 4 ounces)

1 cup pure maple syrup

½ cup bourbon

12 dry-packed diver scallops (each approximately the size of a silver dollar), cleaned

1 tablespoon minced shallots

2 tablespoons chopped fresh chives

1. Bring 4 cups of water to a boil over medium-high heat and season lightly with salt. Add the oats and stir until the mixture starts to thicken. Reduce the heat to low and simmer for about 30 minutes, or until the oats are fully hydrated and tender. Fold in the milk and a nub (about a tablespoon) of butter and season to taste with salt and pepper. Remove from the heat and cover to keep warm.

2. Preheat the oven to 350°F.

3. Spread the butternut squash across the bottom of a roasting pan and sprinkle with 1 tablespoon of the oil. Tuck a sprig of sage and thyme among the squash. Season with salt and pepper and roast, uncovered, for 12 to 15 minutes, or until the squash is fork-tender.

4. Transfer the squash to a blender. Add the chicken stock and puree until smooth. Strain the mixture through a fine-mesh sieve or chinois. Reserve the squash puree in the strainer. (For a more rustic, slightly thicker sauce, the squash and stock can be pureed in a food processor and not strained.)

5. In a 12-quart pot, bring 1 gallon of heavily salted water to a boil. Put a bowl of cold water and ice cubes nearby. Meanwhile, tear the chard leaves from the center rib. Stack the leaves and coarsely chop them. Dice the stems. Boil the leaves for about 1 minute, lift them from the pot with a slotted spoon, and immediately dunk them in the ice bath to stop the cooking. Remove the leaves from the ice bath and set aside. Put the stems in the boiling water and cook for about 30 seconds. Shock them in the ice bath, too, and set them aside separately from the leaves.

6. In a deep, heavy saucepan, combine the maple syrup, bourbon, and remaining sprig thyme and bring to a gentle simmer over low heat. Simmer for about 15 minutes, or until the alcohol has cooked off and the syrup has reduced slightly and thickened. Take care; if the heat is too high the alcohol could ignite. Very carefully remove the thyme. Whisk in 1 tablespoon of the butter until emulsified and smooth. Remove from the heat and cover to keep warm.

7. Heat a large cast-iron skillet or sauté pan over high heat and pour in the remaining 3 tablespoons oil.

8. Gently pat the scallops dry with a paper towel. Season them with salt. When the oil is hot, carefully put the scallops in the pan. Cook for 2 minutes without moving them. Once the edges start to brown, gently flip them over and cook for about 30 seconds longer. Add the remaining sprig of sage and 1 tablespoon of the butter. When the butter melts, use it to baste the scallops, cooking them for about 2 minutes on each side, or until they are golden brown. Remove the scallops from the pan and let them drain on a tray or plate lined with paper towels.

9. In a small saucepan, melt the remaining butter and stir in the shallots. Add the reserved chard leaves and stems and season to taste with salt and pepper.

10. Spoon some oatmeal in the center of each of four serving plates. Top with the Swiss chard and then arrange 3 scallops on top of each serving. Spoon the squash puree around the oatmeal and drizzle a little maple-bourbon glaze over the scallops. Garnish with chives and serve right away. Pass any extra sauce on the side.

Crab Cakes with Charred Corn Rémoulade {SERVES 3 TO 4; MAKES 10 CRAB CAKES}

CRABS AND JUST-PICKED SWEET CORN rule the day during a Maryland summer, where my mother's family is from, and so I'm pleased to showcase both. We usually look for Silver Queen at the farmers' market—an especially sweet hybrid—but any sweet corn is a summertime joy. It takes a lot of crab to make a crab cake and, as I learned the old-fashioned way, picking crabs is a lesson in patience. Fortunately, you can buy crabmeat already picked and ready to go.

PREP TIME: **ABOUT 15 MINUTES**
COOKING TIME: **10 TO 12 MINUTES**

6 tablespoons olive oil

½ cup corn kernels

2 celery stalks, diced

1 small onion, diced

1 small red bell pepper, seeded and diced

1 garlic clove, minced

3 large scallops

3 tablespoons heavy cream

3 large egg whites

Salt

¼ cup mayonnaise

2 teaspoons Dijon mustard

1 pound lump crabmeat, picked over

1 cup crushed oyster crackers

2 tablespoons minced fresh chives

1 tablespoon minced fresh tarragon

1 tablespoon chopped flat-leaf parsley

1 tablespoon fresh lemon juice

2 teaspoons hot sauce (I like Crystal or Tapatío hot sauce)

¼ teaspoon Old Bay Seasoning

2 large eggs, lightly beaten

1 cup dried bread crumbs

3 to 4 tablespoons vegetable oil

Charred Corn Rémoulade (recipe follows)

1. In a large sauté pan, heat the olive oil over medium-high heat. When hot, sauté the corn kernels, celery, onion, bell pepper, and garlic for 5 to 6 minutes, or until the vegetables soften and are aromatic. Remove the pan from the heat and let the vegetables cool.

2. In the bowl of a food processor fitted with the metal blade, pulse the scallops until smooth. Add the cream, egg whites, and a pinch of salt. Pulse until the mousse is fully emulsified and creamy white.

3. In a large bowl, fold the mayonnaise and mustard into the scallop mousse, then fold in the cooled vegetables. Mix in the crabmeat, oyster crackers, chives, tarragon, parsley, lemon juice, hot sauce, and Old Bay Seasoning. Season with salt.

4. Place the beaten eggs in one bowl and the bread crumbs in another. Divide the crab mixture into 10 portions and form into balls. Roll the balls in the beaten eggs and then in the bread crumbs until evenly coated. Gently press the balls into flattened cakes.

5. Heat a few tablespoons of vegetable oil in the sauté pan over medium-high heat. Panfry the crab cakes for about 3 minutes on each side, or until golden brown. Drain the crab cakes on paper towels and serve with the rémoulade on the side.

Charred Corn Rémoulade {MAKES ABOUT 2½ CUPS}

PREP TIME: ABOUT 5 MINUTES, PLUS CHILLING

1¼ cups mayonnaise

1 cup grilled corn kernels (see page 80)

3 tablespoons Dijon mustard

1 tablespoon stone-ground grainy mustard

1 tablespoon prepared horseradish

1 tablespoon chopped flat-leaf parsley

1 tablespoon minced fresh chives

1 tablespoon chopped fresh tarragon

1 tablespoon apple cider vinegar

2 teaspoons hot sauce

1 teaspoon sugar

¼ teaspoon smoked paprika

¼ teaspoon cayenne pepper

1 fresh Fresno chile or jalapeño, seeded and minced

1 shallot, minced

1 garlic clove, minced

Grated zest and juice of 1 lemon

Salt

In a glass, ceramic, or other nonreactive bowl, mix all the ingredients except the lemon zest, lemon juice, and salt. Stir and then season with the lemon zest, lemon juice, and salt. Refrigerate the rémoulade for 1 hour for the flavors to meld.

Lobster Schnitzel with Shaved Asparagus and Citrus Vinaigrette {SERVES 4}

WHO'D HAVE THOUGHT YOU COULD MAKE schnitzel with lobster? It's usually made with pork, chicken, or veal, but I've applied the technique to lobster with a happy outcome. This is a little tricky because you have to butterfly the cooked lobster tails, but since they're already cooked, by the time they hit the pan they need only minutes to "schnitzel" to a crispy crust.

I like to serve this with three different colors of asparagus: green, white, and purple. I don't cook the purple asparagus because when it's heated it turns green. Sort of defeats the purpose. On the other hand, don't spend all day searching for purple asparagus. It's often sold at farmers' markets, so if you see it, grab it. Otherwise, use just green and white, or all green.

PREP TIME: **ABOUT 40 MINUTES**
COOKING TIME: **6 TO 8 MINUTES**

4 cooked lobster tails

2 cups all-purpose flour

2 large eggs, lightly beaten

4 cups panko bread crumbs

3 Meyer lemons, or small common lemons, if Meyers are not available

1 shallot, minced

1 garlic clove, minced

¼ cup extra-virgin olive oil

Salt and freshly ground black pepper

3 ounces green asparagus

3 ounces white asparagus

3 ounces purple asparagus

1 cup half-and-half

8 ounces (2 sticks) unsalted butter

1. Crack the lobster tails open using claw crackers or your hands and remove the tail meat in one piece. Cut the lobster tail meat so that you can butterfly it and all 4 lie flat on the countertop.

2. Put the flour in one shallow dish, the eggs in another, and the bread crumbs in a third. Toss the butterflied lobster tails in the flour to coat. Dip the tails in the egg, turning to coat on both sides, and then in the bread crumbs, making sure they're completely coated. Set aside.

3. Peel 2 of the lemons and divide them into segments. Squeeze the juice of the remaining lemon into a small bowl. Add the shallot, garlic, and oil to the juice and whisk to combine. Season with salt and pepper.

4. Bring a large saucepan of lightly salted water to a boil over medium-high heat. Set a bowl of cold water and ice cubes near the stove. Blanch 2 green asparagus spears and 2 white asparagus spears in the boiling water for about 2 minutes. Lift the asparagus spears from the pan and submerge in the ice bath to cool.

5. When cool, transfer the blanched green asparagus spears to the bowl of a food processor fitted with the metal blade. Add ½ cup of the half-and-half and puree until smooth. Transfer the puree to a bowl. Repeat with the blanched white asparagus spears and remaining half-and-half and transfer to a separate bowl.

6. Shave the remaining spears of green and white asparagus, as well as the purple asparagus spears (if you were able to find them). Use a vegetable peeler to make long ribbons, including the tips of the asparagus. (If it's easier, slice the tips in half and then add them to the shaved spears.) Transfer the shavings to a large bowl and add the lemon segments. Whisk the vinaigrette and drizzle over the salad. Season with salt and pepper and toss to combine.

7. In a deep sauté pan, melt the butter over medium-low heat and cook until it turns nutty brown. Sauté the butterflied lobster tails for 2 minutes on each side, until heated through. Put a lobster "schnitzel" in the center of each of four serving plates and top with the asparagus salad. Spoon the asparagus purees around the lobster and serve.

Lollapalooza Lobster Corn Dogs
{SERVES 12; MAKES 12 CORN DOGS}

WE EASILY SELL MORE than fifteen thousand of these "corn dogs" at Chicago's annual Lollapalooza, a three-day music festival celebrated in Grant Park. That's right: fifteen thousand. I have been the festival's culinary director since 2010, and in the spirit of creating a "state fair atmosphere," I decided to remix the lowly corn dog using one of the world's most luxurious ingredients. They have become the signature dish of the festival, and as far as I am concerned are a sort of culinary Christmas—they are that good and that special.

For the home cook, I suggest using whole lobster tails, although at Lollapalooza we use chopped tail meat bound together with Activa GS, which is not readily available in supermarkets. You could also make these with mild, flaky fin fish, such as haddock or cod. And by the way, the lemony aioli could easily become your go-to "alongside sauce" for fish and seafood.

PREP TIME: **ABOUT 15 MINUTES, PLUS CHILLING**
COOKING TIME: **10 TO 15 MINUTES**

12 cooked lobster tails (from 1-pound lobsters), about 4 ounces each, or similar-sized cooked claw meat

2 cups all-purpose flour

2 cups yellow cornmeal

2 teaspoons baking powder

1 teaspoon cayenne pepper

½ teaspoon baking soda

1 (16-ounce) can creamed corn

3 cups buttermilk

⅔ cup grated onion (from about 1 onion)

1 tablespoon honey

About 2 quarts canola oil, for frying

About 1 cup cornstarch, for coating

Lemon Aioli (recipe follows)

1. Refrigerate the lobster tails for at least 3 hours and up to 12 hours. Skewer each lobster tail as you would skewer a hot dog, inserting a wooden skewer in the large end and threading it through to the narrow end.

2. In a medium bowl, stir the flour, cornmeal, baking powder, cayenne, and baking soda. In another bowl, stir the corn, buttermilk, onion, and honey. Add the flour mixture to the corn mixture and stir to combine. The batter will be a little lumpy.

3. Pour the oil in a deep, heavy pot and heat over medium-high heat until it registers 375°F on a deep-fry thermometer.

4. Put the cornstarch in a shallow dish. Working with a few lobster tails at a time, gently turn them in the cornstarch to coat. Dip the coated lobster tails in the buttermilk batter and then carefully drop the battered tails into the hot oil. The skewers will stick out of the top of the oil. Fry for 4 to 5 minutes, or until crispy and golden. Using tongs, gently lift the lobster corn dogs from the hot oil and drain on paper towels.

5. Let the oil return to temperature and fry the remaining lobster corn dogs. Serve with the lemon aioli.

Lemon Aioli {MAKES ABOUT 2 CUPS}

PREP TIME: **5 TO 10 MINUTES**

¼ cup fresh lemon juice
(from 1 to 2 lemons)

1 tablespoon minced shallot

1 teaspoon chopped garlic

2 cups mayonnaise

Salt and freshly ground black pepper

Paprika

About 2 tablespoons chopped flat-leaf
parsley or chives

1. In a blender, puree the lemon juice, shallots, and garlic.

2. Put the mayonnaise in a small bowl and fold in the puree until well blended. Season with salt and pepper. Garnish with a sprinkling of paprika and the parsley. Serve right away.

Caribbean Shrimp Ceviche with Mango Salsa {SERVES 4}

EATING THIS CEVICHE is like sitting down to a meal with Bob Marley himself. The recipe title alone makes me think of sand, sun, and blue waves breaking gently on a crescent sliver of beach. Ceviche means cooking without heat, allowing the acid in the marinade to break down the proteins in the shrimp (or other seafood) so that the end result is the same as if it were cooked with heat. It's a popular way to prepare seafood in warm countries where it's not much fun to heat up the kitchen.

For this dish, use shrimp or substitute octopus, lobster, or your favorite fin fish. Same for the mango in the salsa—try another tropical fruit, such as papaya, pineapple, passion fruit, or guava. Plantains are another product of the tropics. They look like bananas and taste something like them, too, although they cannot be eaten raw. They are not sweet, either, so you need to sweeten or flavor them with savory seasonings. The most common preparation is to mash them, which is great, but here I fry them for plantain chips. Season them as soon as you take them from the pan so that the salt will stick to the still warm and slightly oil-slicked plantains.

PREP TIME: ABOUT 20 MINUTES, PLUS STANDING
COOKING TIME: 2 TO 3 MINUTES

PLANTAIN CHIPS

Vegetable oil, for frying

1 plantain, peeled and thinly sliced crosswise into rounds

Salt

MANGO SALSA

½ cup chopped mango

3 tablespoons chopped cilantro

2 tablespoons fresh lime juice

½ jalapeño, seeded and chopped

Salt

CEVICHE

1 pound peeled and deveined Laughing Bird shrimp (see Note)

2 cups fresh lime juice (from 8 to 10 limes)

½ cup minced cilantro

½ red onion, thinly sliced

1 garlic clove, minced

1 teaspoon salt

WHIPPED AVOCADO

1 avocado, peeled and cut into chunks

1 garlic clove, coarsely chopped

½ bunch cilantro, coarsely chopped

3 tablespoons fresh lime juice

Salt

1. For the plantain chips, pour enough oil into a large, heavy, deep saucepan to reach a depth of 3 inches. Heat over medium-high heat until it registers 350°F on a deep-fry thermometer.

2. Carefully drop the plantain slices into the hot oil and fry for about 90 seconds, or until the plantain chips are crisp and golden brown.

3. Using tongs, lift the plantain chips from the hot oil and spread them out on paper towels to drain. Season with salt. Set aside.

4. For the mango salsa, in a glass, ceramic, or other nonreactive dish, gently stir the mango, cilantro, lime juice, and jalapeño. Season with salt and set aside.

5. For the ceviche, in a glass, ceramic, or other nonreactive dish, stir the shrimp, lime juice, cilantro, onion, garlic, and salt. Set aside at room temperature for about 20 minutes, or until the shrimp are firm.

6. For the whipped avocado, combine the avocado with the garlic, cilantro, and lime juice in a blender and puree until smooth. Season with salt and pulse to combine.

7. Drain the excess lime juice from the shrimp and discard.

8. Serve the ceviche with the salsa, avocado, and plantain chips on the side.

NOTE: Laughing Bird shrimp are plump, tasty, farmed shrimp that are raised under the best circumstances for farmed crustaceans: filtered Caribbean water and a vegetarian diet. If you cannot get Laughing Bird shrimp, buy the best, freshest shrimp you can find.

Steamed Mussels with Mexican Chorizo and Cerveza {SERVES 4 TO 6}

MY CHEF-PARTNER MERLIN VERRIER came up with this one, and it's a home run! Mussels, beer, and chorizo—what more needs to be said? Merlin is a laid-back California dude who approaches cooking with that relaxed West Coast attitude, and the world is a better place for it. You can make this more of a meal by adding hominy (posole), escarole, and tomatoes.

PREP TIME: **ABOUT 15 MINUTES**
COOKING TIME: **ABOUT 10 MINUTES**

2 tablespoons vegetable oil

4 ounces Mexican chorizo (see Note)

½ small red onion, thinly sliced

3 garlic cloves, finely sliced

1½ teaspoons chopped fresh oregano

3 pounds bouchot mussels, PEI mussels, or other high-quality farmed mussels, cleaned

½ cup diced tomatoes

½ cup diced tomatillos

2 fresh or dried bay leaves

3 cans Tecate beer or other pale lager

Juice of ½ orange

Juice of 1 lime

8 tablespoons (1 stick) unsalted butter

Hot sauce (I like Tapatío and Crystal hot sauce)

Salt

¼ cup chopped cilantro

2 radishes, trimmed and shaved

1 jalapeño, seeded and thinly sliced

1. In a large, deep pot, heat the oil over medium-high heat. When shimmering hot, brown the chorizo for 4 to 5 minutes, or until cooked through.

2. Pour out the excess oil, or carefully wipe out the pot with paper towels, leaving the chorizo and enough oil in the pot to cook the onion and garlic.

3. Add the onion, garlic, and oregano and cook, stirring, for 1 minute. Add the mussels, tomatoes, tomatillos, and bay leaves. Stir to combine and then add the beer. Cover the pot and let the mussels steam for 2 to 3 minutes, or until they open.

4. Add the orange juice, lime juice, and butter. Heat until the butter melts and season to taste with hot sauce and salt. Remove and discard the bay leaves. Garnish with the cilantro, radishes, and jalapeño.

NOTE: What's the difference between Mexican and Spanish chorizo sausage? Both are totally addictive pork sausages with spicy, smoky flavors but the Mexican sausage always needs to be cooked before you can serve it. Spanish chorizo is usually cured before it's sold and so, like other charcuterie, can be sliced and munched without cooking.

5
DOWN on the FARM

Kung Pao Drumsticks with
Ginger Honey and Toasted
Peanuts

Sesame Chicken Thighs with Bok
Choy and Plums

Grilled Chicken with
Watermelon-Olive Salsa

Duck Confit Agnolotti with Kale
and Pine Nuts

Roasted Quail with Wild
Mushrooms and Fava Beans

Roasted Pheasant with Tuscan
Kale and Hazelnuts

Wild Turkey with Cranberry
Compote and Glazed Chestnuts

New York Strip Steak with
Mushrooms and Blue Cheese

The GrahamBurger

Grilled Skirt Steak with
Black Beans and Chimichurri

Filet Mignon with Creamed
Spinach and Watercress

Short Rib Stroganoff with
Spaetzle, Wild Mushrooms,
and Peppered Sour Cream

Mom's Brisket Pot Roast

Pork Chops with Sweet Potato
Latkes and Cinnamon-Spiced Apples

Roasted Goat with Salsa Verde
and Grilled Onions

Yogurt-Marinated Leg of Lamb
with Crushed Olive Oil Potatoes
and Grainy Mustard

OKAY, SO LET'S ALL agree that it's a cliché to say you cook "farm to table." It's a given nowadays that chefs wanna use the best products available, but we also want to make sure those foods are raised and slaughtered as humanely as possible—and so many of us do indeed cook "farm to table."

And yet, whether it's beef, pork, lamb, chicken, or another meat, many cooks and eaters don't know or perhaps don't *want* to know where their meat comes from. The fact is that an animal gave its life (not a voluntary choice) so that you or I could create something delicious. This is why I feel strongly that we show them the respect they deserve.

The way you cut, season, tie, grill, sauté, braise, or roast is of equal importance. Just keep remembering Wilbur from *Charlotte's Web*, saying he doesn't want to go the way of all pigs. I promise that you'll feel enough guilt so that you will never again let your steak burn on the grill or your chicken dry out in the oven. Respect the ingredients!

Kung Pao Drumsticks with Ginger Honey and Toasted Peanuts

{SERVES 4}

I TRY TO STAY TRUE TO CLASSIC kung pao chicken in this recipe, although I make it with legs rather than breasts because of the richer flavor of the dark meat. I spice it up with sambal chili sauce, which is nicely warm but not burning.

PREP TIME: **5 TO 10 MINUTES**
COOKING TIME: **23 TO 30 MINUTES**

½ cup honey

2 tablespoons minced fresh ginger

4 cups canola oil, plus 1 to 2 tablespoons

1 tablespoon minced shallot

1 garlic clove, minced

1½ teaspoons rice wine vinegar

1 teaspoon mirin

1½ teaspoons dark soy sauce

1 teaspoon hoisin

½ teaspoon sambal chili sauce

3 scallions, minced

½ cup chopped toasted salted peanuts (see Note)

4 trimmed chicken drumsticks (legs)

1. Put the honey and 1 tablespoon of the ginger in a saucepan and bring to a simmer over low heat. Cook gently for about 5 minutes to infuse the honey with the ginger. Strain the sauce through a chinois or fine-mesh sieve into a bowl. Cover and set aside.

2. In another saucepan, heat 1 tablespoon of the oil over medium-high heat. Sauté the shallot, garlic, and remaining 1 tablespoon ginger for 1 to 2 minutes, or until the shallot is translucent. Add the vinegar and mirin and bring to a rapid simmer. Cook for 30 seconds or until reduced by half. Add the soy sauce, hoisin, and chili sauce and simmer for 5 minutes longer, or until the sauce begins to thicken. Strain the sauce into a shallow bowl.

3. In another bowl, toss the scallions with the peanuts.

4. In a heavy pot, heat the 4 cups oil until it registers 350°F on a deep-fry thermometer.

5. Using tongs, submerge the chicken legs in the hot oil. Do not crowd the pot (you may have to fry the chicken in two batches if the pot is not large). Fry for 5 to 8 minutes, or until the juices run clear when you remove a leg from the oil and pierce its meatiest section with a small, sharp knife. If not done, return the leg to the oil and cook for 2 to 3 minutes longer. When done, use tongs to remove the legs and set aside on a paper towel–lined plate.

6. Put the hot drumsticks in the bowl with the shallot-mirin sauce and toss to coat. Transfer to the bowl with the peanuts and scallions and roll to coat. Drizzle with the ginger sauce.

NOTE: To toast the peanuts, spread them in a dry skillet and cook over medium-high heat for about 1 minute, shaking the pan a few times, until lightly browned. Cool on a plate.

Sesame Chicken Thighs with Bok Choy and Plums {SERVES 6}

INSPIRED BY JAPANESE COOKING, these chicken thighs are very simple. The flavors of the other ingredients work so well, you won't want to mess with them—unless you want to prove something! Bok choy, plums, and ginger play so nicely together that you will be completely satisfied. But if you wanted to change it up a bit, make a salad of those ingredients, or better yet, make the dish and then serve the salad the next day with the leftovers.

PREP TIME: **ABOUT 20 MINUTES**
COOKING TIME: **30 TO 35 MINUTES**

CHICKEN THIGHS

Peanut oil

1 tablespoon minced garlic

1 tablespoon minced shallot

1 tablespoon minced fresh ginger

2 tablespoons sambal chili sauce

1 tablespoon soy sauce

½ cup rice wine vinegar

¼ cup mirin

2 tablespoons honey

1 teaspoon fish sauce

1 teaspoon Sriracha

1 tablespoon sugar

1 tablespoon fresh lime juice

1 teaspoon minced fresh chives

1 teaspoon minced cilantro

1½ teaspoons finely chopped lime zest

1 tablespoon black sesame seeds

6 bone-in chicken thighs, preferably organic

Salt and freshly ground black pepper

1 tablespoon olive oil

BOK CHOY AND PLUMS

1 tablespoon olive oil

2 teaspoons soy sauce (I recommend aged soy sauce)

2 teaspoons sesame oil

3 heads bok choy, trimmed

4 plums, pitted and sliced

1 tablespoon toasted sesame seeds (see Note)

Salt

1. For the chicken, pour enough peanut oil into a saucepan to cover the bottom and heat over medium-high heat. Cook the garlic, shallot, ginger, and chili sauce, stirring, just until aromatic. Add the soy sauce and stir to scrape up any bits sticking to the pan. Add the vinegar, mirin, honey, fish sauce, and Sriracha and bring to a gentle simmer.

2. Dissolve the sugar in the lime juice and add to the pan. Simmer the glaze for 4 to 5 minutes, until it comes together.

3. Fold in the chives, cilantro, lime zest, and sesame seeds. Stir to mix and then remove the pan from the heat. Set the glaze aside, covered, until needed.

4. Season the chicken thighs with salt and pepper and rub them with olive oil.

5. Prepare a gas or charcoal grill so that the heating elements or coals are medium-hot. If possible, use wood to cook this dish.

6. Grill the thighs for 8 to 10 minutes on each side, brushing them several times with the glaze. When the thighs are cooked through, dunk them in the glaze and then return them to the grill. Cook for a minute or two, or until the skin is charred and tacky.

7. Meanwhile, for the bok choy and plums, in a large bowl, whisk the olive oil, soy sauce, and sesame oil. Add the bok choy and toss them with the dressing.

8. Put the bok choy on the grill and cook for about 2 minutes, or until the leaves begin to wilt and char. Using tongs, remove the bok choy from the grill and toss them in a bowl with the plums and sesame seeds. Season with salt.

9. Serve the thighs with the bok choy placed on top.

NOTE: To toast the sesame seeds, spread them in a small, dry skillet and toast over medium heat for 45 to 60 seconds until they turn a shade darker and are aromatic. Take care that they don't burn.

Grilled Chicken with Watermelon-Olive Salsa {SERVES 4 TO 6}

ALL I GOTTA DO is read the title of this recipe and I start humming "Summertime" by DJ Jazzy Jeff & the Fresh Prince. And why not? Chicken, watermelon salsa, the grill. . . . Makes me reach for my "World's Best Cook" apron (a must-have gift for every dad's first Father's Day) and get cookin'!

PREP TIME: **ABOUT 40 MINUTES, PLUS MARINATING**
COOKING TIME: **ABOUT 40 MINUTES**

CHICKEN

- 2 (2½- to 3-pound) whole chickens
- Salt and freshly ground black pepper
- 1 tablespoon piment d'Espelette, cayenne pepper, or hot paprika
- 1 teaspoon ground sumac (optional)
- 1 tablespoon cumin seeds
- 1 teaspoon fennel seeds
- 1 teaspoon poppy seeds
- 2 cups plain yogurt
- 6 garlic cloves
- 1 tablespoon honey
- 1 teaspoon red pepper flakes
- 2 tablespoons chopped fresh oregano leaves
- 2 tablespoons chopped flat-leaf parsley
- Zest of 1 lemon

WATERMELON-OLIVE SALSA

- 2 tablespoons rice wine vinegar
- 2 tablespoons olive oil
- 1 tablespoon honey
- 2 teaspoons ground sumac (optional)
- 3 cups diced watermelon
- 1 small red onion, thinly sliced
- 1 cucumber, peeled and diced
- ½ cup chopped kalamata olives
- 1 jalapeño, thinly sliced (and seeded if you like less heat)
- ½ cup chopped flat-leaf parsley
- ¼ cup coarsely chopped cilantro leaves
- ¼ cup coarsely chopped mint leaves
- Grated zest and juice of 1 lime
- Salt

1. Trim any excess skin from around the necks and cavities of the chickens. Using poultry shears, carefully remove the backbones. Season the chickens on both sides with salt and pepper.

2. Put the piment d'Espelette, sumac, cumin seeds, fennel seeds, and poppy seeds in a spice grinder and process to a powder. Transfer to a blender and add the yogurt, garlic, honey, red pepper flakes, oregano, parsley, and lemon zest and blend until well mixed.

3. Lay the chickens in a glass or ceramic dish large enough to hold them in a single layer, or put them in a large resealable plastic bag. Cover them with the yogurt marinade, turning them to coat thoroughly. Refrigerate for at least 2 hours and up to 8 hours.

4. Prepare a charcoal or gas grill for indirect grilling so that the coals or heating elements are medium-hot.

5. Lift the chickens from the marinade and let the excess drip back into the dish or plastic bag. Scrape off any that does not drip off. Lay the chickens on the grill, skin side up, spread out so they are as flat as possible. Cover the grill and brush the chickens with the marinade every 10 minutes or so. Cook for about 40 minutes, or until the juices run clear when the dark meat is pierced in a thick place and the internal temperature of the white meat is 165°F.

6. Meanwhile, for the watermelon-olive salsa, in a large bowl, whisk the vinegar, oil, honey, and sumac.

7. Add the watermelon, onion, cucumber, olives, jalapeño, parsley, cilantro, and mint. Toss gently to coat with the dressing. Season with the lime zest and lime juice, taste, and adjust the seasoning with salt. Serve with the chicken.

Duck Confit Agnolotti with Kale and Pine Nuts {SERVES 6}

MAN, I LOVE DUCK confit! What a cool technique: preserving meat in its own fat. You can cure it yourself, or buy the confit from a good butcher (ask ahead). Serving this with kale and pine nuts kicks up the flavor and texture. If you don't feel like making your own agnolotti, serve this with pappardelle. A lot easier and just as good.

PREP TIME: 45 TO 50 MINUTES, PLUS CHILLING
COOKING TIME: ABOUT 10 MINUTES

PASTA DOUGH

- 1¾ cups all-purpose flour, plus more for dusting
- 6 large egg yolks
- 1 large egg
- 1 tablespoon olive oil

FILLING

- 12 ounces mascarpone cheese (about 1½ cups)
- 2 large egg yolks
- 2 shallots, minced
- Grated zest of 1 orange
- Grated zest of 1 lemon
- 1 pound duck confit meat (see Note)
- 1 tablespoon minced flat-leaf parsley
- Salt and freshly ground black pepper
- Semolina flour, for dusting
- 1 large egg

KALE

- ½ cup olive oil
- 1 garlic clove, sliced
- ½ teaspoon red pepper flakes
- 6 ounces (1½ sticks) unsalted butter
- 1 bunch kale (8 to 10 ounces), ribs removed and leaves trimmed
- Juice of 1 lemon
- Salt
- 1 tablespoon minced flat-leaf parsley
- 1 ounce ricotta salata, shaved (about ¼ cup)
- ½ cup pine nuts, toasted

1. For the pasta dough, put the flour in a large bowl and make a well in the center. Add the egg yolks, egg, and oil to the well. Pull the flour from around the sides of the well into the wet ingredients, gently breaking up the eggs with your fingers. Work around the circle formed by the flour and the well until the dough resembles a sticky paste.

2. Turn the dough out onto a lightly floured surface and knead gently until the dough is smooth and bounces back slightly when you press it with your finger. Form the dough into a ball and wrap well with plastic wrap. Refrigerate for at least 20 minutes to allow the dough to relax. The dough can be refrigerated until needed, up to 4 hours.

3. For the filling, in a large bowl, whisk the mascarpone, egg yolks, shallots, orange zest, and lemon zest. Fold in the duck confit and parsley and season with salt and pepper.

4. Using a pasta machine, roll the pasta through the #2 setting to make four 18-inch-long strips. Lay the strips on a lightly floured surface.

5. Whisk the egg with 2 tablespoons of water to make an egg wash. Brush the exposed side of the pasta strips with the egg wash.

6. Dollop 2 to 3 tablespoons of filling down the length of 2 strips of the pasta, about 1½ inches apart. Top with the remaining sheets of pasta. Brush the pasta with egg wash. Press or pinch between each mound of filling to make little pillows, each measuring 1 inch by 2½ inches. With a pastry wheel or sharp knife, separate each agnolotti and dust with semolina. You should have about 24 agnolotti.

7. For the kale, in a large skillet, heat the oil over medium-high heat. Cook the garlic and red pepper flakes for about 1 minute, just to toast them. Add the butter and when it melts, let it cook a little longer so it begins to brown. Toss the kale into the skillet and turn it to coat with the browned butter. Cook for 4 to 5 minutes to give the kale time to wilt, and season to taste with a little lemon juice (you may not need all the juice) and salt.

8. Meanwhile, bring a pot of lightly salted water to a boil. Drop the agnolotti into the water and let them cook for 2 to 3 minutes, or until they bob to the surface. Lift the agnolotti from the water with a slotted spoon.

9. Divide the kale and pasta among six serving plates. Sprinkle with parsley, ricotta salata, and pine nuts and serve.

NOTE: Ask your butcher for duck confit meat. It should be picked through and in small pieces. If your butcher can't get it for you, substitute chicken leg confit or braised chicken legs.

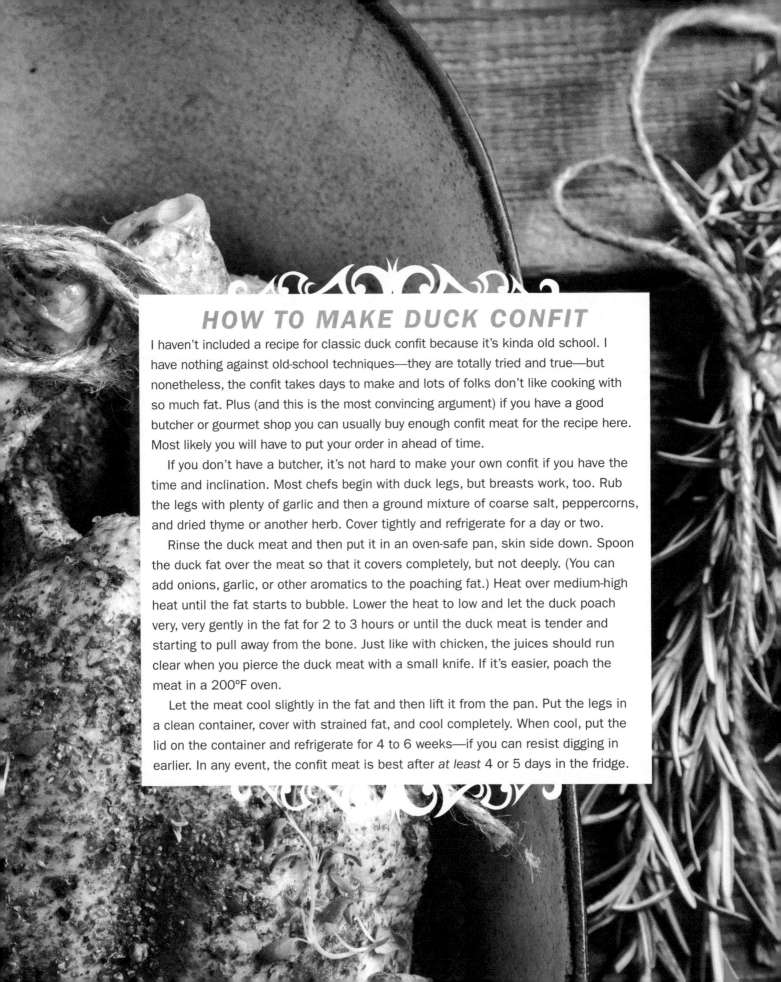

HOW TO MAKE DUCK CONFIT

I haven't included a recipe for classic duck confit because it's kinda old school. I have nothing against old-school techniques—they are totally tried and true—but nonetheless, the confit takes days to make and lots of folks don't like cooking with so much fat. Plus (and this is the most convincing argument) if you have a good butcher or gourmet shop you can usually buy enough confit meat for the recipe here. Most likely you will have to put your order in ahead of time.

If you don't have a butcher, it's not hard to make your own confit if you have the time and inclination. Most chefs begin with duck legs, but breasts work, too. Rub the legs with plenty of garlic and then a ground mixture of coarse salt, peppercorns, and dried thyme or another herb. Cover tightly and refrigerate for a day or two.

Rinse the duck meat and then put it in an oven-safe pan, skin side down. Spoon the duck fat over the meat so that it covers completely, but not deeply. (You can add onions, garlic, or other aromatics to the poaching fat.) Heat over medium-high heat until the fat starts to bubble. Lower the heat to low and let the duck poach very, very gently in the fat for 2 to 3 hours or until the duck meat is tender and starting to pull away from the bone. Just like with chicken, the juices should run clear when you pierce the duck meat with a small knife. If it's easier, poach the meat in a 200°F oven.

Let the meat cool slightly in the fat and then lift it from the pan. Put the legs in a clean container, cover with strained fat, and cool completely. When cool, put the lid on the container and refrigerate for 4 to 6 weeks—if you can resist digging in earlier. In any event, the confit meat is best after *at least* 4 or 5 days in the fridge.

Roasted Quail with Wild Mushrooms and Fava Beans {SERVES 6}

WHEN I LIVED IN VERMONT and had the chance to run my first kitchen at the Jackson House Inn and Restaurant in Woodstock, I was blessed to have access to the most incredible products. Quail fell firmly in this category, and we received it at the kitchen door as fresh as could be. I'm pretty sure it was killed the day I ordered it. Serving it simply with fava beans and wild, foraged morel mushrooms (without liver but *with* a nice Chianti) perfectly showcases the yummy, tiny birdie. You can make this springtime dish with chicken, if it's easier (which it is!).

PREP TIME: **ABOUT 10 MINUTES**
COOKING TIME: **20 TO 25 MINUTES**

QUAIL

- 6 semiboneless whole quail
- Salt and freshly ground black pepper
- Zest of 2 lemons, cut into pieces
- 6 sprigs fresh thyme
- 6 garlic cloves, unpeeled
- 3 tablespoons unsalted butter, cut into 6 pieces
- Olive oil

MUSHROOMS AND FAVA BEANS

- About ½ cup olive oil
- 2 shallots, minced
- 2 garlic cloves, minced
- ½ teaspoon red pepper flakes
- 12 ounces wild mushrooms (such as chanterelles, morels, beech, or hen of the woods), trimmed
- 1 tablespoon fresh thyme leaves
- ½ cup dry sherry
- 1 teaspoon sherry vinegar
- Salt
- 1 cup peeled shelled fava beans
- 3 tablespoons unsalted butter
- 1 tablespoon chopped flat-leaf parsley

1. For the quail, preheat the oven to 400°F. Arrange the oven racks so a roasting pan can sit on the top rack.

2. Season the quail all over with salt and pepper. Put a piece of lemon zest, a sprig of thyme, a clove of garlic, and a cube of butter in the cavity of each quail. Truss closed with kitchen twine.

3. Arrange the quail in a roasting pan and drizzle generously with oil. Roast for about 18 minutes, or until the skin is golden and the juices run clear.

4. For the mushrooms and favas, in a large skillet, heat the oil over medium heat. Add the shallots, garlic, and red pepper flakes and cook for 20 seconds. Add the mushrooms, raise the heat to medium-high, and sauté the mushrooms for about 4 minutes, or until they soften and caramelize. Add the thyme to the pan and then deglaze the pan with the sherry and the sherry vinegar, scraping up any browned bits sticking to the pan. Cook until the liquid has been absorbed.

5. Meanwhile, bring a pot of lightly salted water to a boil. Add the fava beans and blanch for 2 to 3 minutes, or until they soften. Drain.

6. Add the fava beans to the skillet with the mushrooms and cook for 30 seconds. Add the butter and parsley, stir to combine, and remove from the heat.

7. Arrange the mushrooms and fava beans on six serving plates and top each with a quail.

Roasted Pheasant with Tuscan Kale and Hazelnuts {SERVES 2}

PHEASANT IS SO COOL. It's like a more flavorful chicken and is a staple in the upper Midwest. My dad was raised in Michigan and tells me stories of hunting pheasants with my grandpa. While I am more of a fisherman and have yet to go hunting (or shoot a gun, for that matter!), I like hearing these stories. In this recipe, I take the pheasant in an Italianesque direction by using kale and hazelnuts—two of my favorite ingredients. You can take this in another direction with another green and different nut to make it your own. After all, recipes are building blocks to provide the cook with a framework in which to create.

PREP TIME: 20 TO 25 MINUTES, PLUS BRINING
COOKING TIME: 1 HOUR 10 MINUTES TO 1 HOUR 25 MINUTES

BRINE

1 cup salt

½ cup sugar

3 cardamom pods

2 fresh bay leaves

6 coriander seeds

6 whole black peppercorns

PHEASANT

1 pheasant (2 to 3 pounds)

1 onion, coarsely chopped

1 carrot, coarsely chopped

1 apple, cored and coarsely chopped

1 parsnip, coarsely chopped

1 leek, white and light green parts only, coarsely chopped

3 garlic cloves, skins on

8 tablespoons (1 stick) unsalted butter, cut into cubes

2 fresh bay leaves, torn

TURNIPS AND KALE

4 medium turnips, cubed

2 bunches Tuscan kale (8 to 10 ounces each), ribs and thick stems removed

1 Honeycrisp apple or similar crisp, sweet apple, cored and diced

1 cup chopped roasted hazelnuts

1 ounce Parmesan cheese, shaved (about ¼ cup)

1 tablespoon apple cider

1 teaspoon apple cider vinegar

Salt and freshly cracked black pepper

1. For the brine, put the salt, sugar, cardamom, bay leaves, coriander, and peppercorns in a large pot. Add about 1 gallon of water and bring to a boil. Adjust the heat and simmer for about 3 minutes to give the sugar time to dissolve and the spices to release their essence. Remove from the heat and strain the brine through a fine-mesh sieve. Discard the herbs and spices and let the brine cool.

2. For the pheasant, when the brine has cooled, submerge the pheasant in the brine and refrigerate for 6 to 8 hours.

3. Preheat the oven to 500ºF.

4. In a large bowl, toss together the onion, carrot, apple, parsnip, leek, and garlic to make a mirepoix.

5. Lift the pheasant from the brine and pat dry with paper towels. Snip the wing tips. Put a handful of mirepoix in the pheasant's cavity. Rub the skin with about half the butter and then put a few cubes of butter inside the bird's cavity.

6. Scatter the remaining mirepoix in a roasting pan. Add the bay leaves and the remaining butter. Set the pheasant on top of the vegetables and roast for 15 minutes to darken and crisp the skin.

7. Lower the oven temperature to 350°F and continue to roast the pheasant for 30 to 45 minutes more, depending on the size of the bird, until the breast meat registers 155°F on an instant-read thermometer. Transfer the pheasant to a serving platter, cover it with aluminum foil, and let it rest while the turnips and kale roast. Discard the mirepoix from the roasting pan. Raise the oven temperature to 375°F.

8. For the turnips and kale, spread the turnips in the roasting pan with the drippings from the pheasant and roast for about 10 minutes. Add the kale and roast for 8 minutes more.

9. Put the contents of the roasting pan in a mixing bowl and add the apple, hazelnuts, Parmesan, apple cider, and vinegar. Stir well and season with salt and pepper.

10. Spoon the vegetables around the pheasant and serve.

Wild Turkey with Cranberry Compote and Glazed Chestnuts {SERVES 6}

HOW MANY OF YOU have ever tasted a wild turkey (and I mean the bird, not the bourbon)? Exactly. Sure, the ungainly birds are much more populous these days than they were sixty years ago—more than six million turkeys now call North America home, as compared to barely five hundred thousand in the 1950s—but that probably won't stop most of you from using a regular ol' turkey for this. And why not? The finished dish will still be tasty. You could also use chicken or even pork, if you're feeling loco.

PREP TIME: **15 TO 20 MINUTES, PLUS CHILLING AND RESTING**
COOKING TIME: **ABOUT 1 HOUR**

CRANBERRY COMPOTE

- 1 pound fresh or frozen cranberries
- 1 blood orange, chopped (leave the skin on the orange)
- 1 cup fresh orange juice (from 3 to 4 oranges)
- ½ cup sugar
- ¼ cup Grand Marnier, Cointreau, or other orange-flavored liqueur
- ¼ cup honey
- 1 cinnamon stick
- Salt

GLAZED CHESTNUTS

- 3 cups chestnuts, peeled and halved
- ¼ cup maple syrup
- 1 sprig fresh sage
- 6 tablespoons (¾ stick) unsalted butter
- Salt

TURKEY BREASTS

- 3 tablespoons olive oil
- 3 wild turkey breasts (about 1½ pounds each)
- Salt and freshly cracked black pepper
- 6 ounces (1½ sticks) unsalted butter
- 2 garlic cloves, unpeeled
- 2 sprigs fresh thyme
- 2 chiles de arbol, or another small, hot chile

1. For the cranberries, in a saucepan, mix the cranberries, orange, orange juice, sugar, liqueur, honey, cinnamon stick, and ½ cup of water. Cook over low heat, stirring regularly, for about 1 hour.

2. Just before it's done, season the sauce with a little salt. Give it a vigorous stir to break up the cranberries and release their flavor.

3. Remove the cinnamon stick and let the sauce cool. The compote is best made a day ahead and refrigerated.

4. For the chestnuts, put the chestnuts, maple syrup, and sage in a sauté pan and heat over medium heat, stirring gently. During this time, the syrup will reduce a little and glaze the chestnuts.

5. Add the butter and stir the chestnuts to coat them with the melting butter. Season with salt.

6. For the turkey, preheat the oven to 375°F.

7. Set two large, oven-safe skillets (large enough to hold the breasts) over medium-high heat. Divide the oil between the skillets, tilting them to coat the bottom of the pans.

8. Liberally season the turkey breasts with salt and pepper. When the oil shimmers, arrange the turkey breasts skin side down in the pans. Cook for about 8 minutes, or until the skin begins to develop a rich, golden color.

9. Distribute the butter, garlic, thyme, and chiles between the pans. Tightly cover both pans with aluminum foil and transfer them to the oven. Roast for about 20 minutes, basting occasionally with the buttery sauce in the bottom of each pan.

10. Remove the turkey breasts from the pans and let them rest, tented with aluminum foil, for about 10 minutes before carving.

11. Serve the turkey with the cranberry compote and glazed chestnuts.

New York Strip Steak with Mushrooms and Blue Cheese {SERVES 4}

STRIP STEAK MAY NOT SOUND as extravagant as filet mignon, but as anyone who has tasted both cuts knows, the former is the tastier of the two. I opt to serve the steak with a simple, down-home potato salad rather than a silken potato puree, and then I pair it with blue cheese and Cabernet jam to add both funkiness and sophistication.

When the steak is done, remember the general rule for resting: half the cooking time. That means a steak that is cooked in 10 minutes on the grill or under the broiler should rest for 5 minutes. During cooking, the juices migrate to the surface and then need resting time to distribute themselves throughout the meat, so that when you slice it, it's seductively juicy through and through.

PREP TIME: **ABOUT 30 MINUTES**
COOKING TIME: **65 TO 70 MINUTES**

- 4 New York strip steaks (about 8 ounces each)
- 2 cups cremini mushrooms, trimmed
- 2 cups peeled pearl onions
- 2 teaspoons salt, plus more as needed
- 2 tablespoons sherry vinegar
- 2 tablespoons unsalted butter
- 4 ounces blue cheese, crumbled (about 1 cup)
- 2 tablespoons olive oil
- Freshly ground black pepper
- Roasted Potato Salad (page 66)
- Cabernet Jam (recipe follows)

1. Remove the fat cap and silverskin from the steaks. Return the steaks to the refrigerator and put the fat in a saucepan. Render (melt) the fat over low heat, which will take about 30 minutes. When rendered, strain the fat through a chinois or fine-mesh sieve into a bowl and set aside. If the steak you buy is already trimmed of fat, use canola oil instead for cooking the veg.

2. Preheat the oven to 350°F.

3. Put 1 tablespoon of the fat (or canola oil) in each of two large sauté pans and heat over high heat. When the fat is very hot and shimmering, put the mushrooms in one pan and the onions in the other. Season both with salt and cook the vegetables over medium heat for 5 to 10 minutes, or until heavily browned.

4. Divide the vinegar and butter between the pans and cook, stirring occasionally, for 2 to 3 minutes, or until the butter melts and the liquid thickens to a glaze. Transfer the mushrooms and onions to a roasting pan and roast for about 10 minutes, or until the vegetables are fully cooked.

5. Transfer the vegetables to a large saucepan (do not turn off the oven) and add the blue cheese. The heat from the vegetables should melt the cheese.

6. Meanwhile, in a large, oven-safe sauté pan (you might need two pans), heat the olive oil over medium-high heat until hot.

7. Season both sides of the steaks with salt and pepper and cook them in the pan(s) for 7 minutes. Turn the steaks and then transfer to the oven and cook for 10 minutes longer for medium-rare meat. Take the steaks from the pan(s) and let them rest on a cutting board for 7 or 8 minutes before slicing.

8. Put a small amount of potato salad on each of four serving plates. Put the sliced meat on the potato salad and then top the meat with the mushrooms and onions. Put a little Cabernet jam on each plate and serve.

Cabernet Jam {MAKES ABOUT 2 CUPS}

PREP TIME: **ABOUT 10 MINUTES**
COOKING TIME: **ABOUT 10 MINUTES**

8 cups red wine

1 cup prunes

1 cup dried cherries

1 cup dried cranberries

1 cup raisins

1. In a large pot, combine the wine, prunes, cherries, cranberries, and raisins. Bring to a boil and then reduce the heat to low and cook slowly for about 10 minutes, or until the mixture has reduced by half.

2. Working in batches, transfer the jam to a blender and puree until thick and smooth. Transfer to a lidded container and refrigerate for up to 2 weeks until ready to serve.

The GrahamBurger {SERVES 4}

WHEN IT COMES TO the GrahamBurger, less is more. Instead of loading a burger with bacon, mushrooms, tomatoes, or whatever else lurks in the refrigerator, I've toned this down by creating a simple patty adorned only with Brie, onions, watercress, and garlic aioli. Nothing more. I've had a million burgers in my life, and I'm pretty confident about this one!

PREP TIME: **ABOUT 15 MINUTES, PLUS MARINATING**
COOKING TIME: **ABOUT 40 MINUTES**

5 garlic cloves

1½ cups olive oil

¼ cup mayonnaise

1 pound ground sirloin beef

4 ounces ground pork

Salt and freshly ground black pepper

1 red onion, cut into ⅛-inch-thick slices

1 cup apple cider vinegar

10 ounces Brie cheese, sliced into 4 thin pieces

4 pretzel rolls

1 bunch upland cress (see Note)

1. Put the garlic cloves and 1 cup of the oil in a small saucepan and simmer over low heat for about 20 minutes, or until the garlic is soft. Lift the garlic from the oil using a slotted spoon and transfer to a blender. Reserve any excess oil for another use. Add the mayonnaise and blend for 2 to 3 minutes, until smooth. Spoon into a small container and refrigerate until needed. The mayo can be refrigerated for up to 5 days.

2. Mix the sirloin and pork and season with salt and pepper. Form into 4 patties, each about ½ inch thick. Refrigerate until ready to grill.

3. Put the onion in a bowl and add the vinegar and remaining ½ cup oil. Season with salt and pepper. Let the onions marinate for at least 30 minutes, but longer if possible, 8 to 10 hours or overnight. (The longer, the better!)

4. Prepare a charcoal or gas grill so that the coals or heating elements are medium-hot.

5. Gently put the onion slices on the grill and cook for 3 minutes on each side. Turn them carefully so they don't slip between the grill grates.

6. Put the burgers on the grill alongside the onions and grill for 7 minutes. Turn them over and grill for 7 minutes longer, or until cooked through. Three minutes before the burgers are done, lay one slice of the Brie on each burger to give it time to melt.

7. Spread the mayonnaise on both sides of the rolls. Top with a cheeseburger and then garnish with the onions and cress. Serve immediately.

NOTE: Upland cress is very similar to watercress but is grown on dry land. Its peppery-tasting leaves are a little stronger than watercress, although one can be substituted for the other for most uses—and certainly the more familiar watercress works well here.

Grilled Skirt Steak with Black Beans and Chimichurri {SERVES 6}

THIS DISH IS INFLUENCED by the cooking of our great Southwest. When I started out, I was lucky enough to spend time working in Dallas, Texas, at Dean Fearing's restaurant, now called the Mansion but then it was the Mansion on Turtle Creek. Dean is an amazing chef and I immediately took to the flavors and cooking techniques of the Southwest, learning that sometimes the best way to elevate ingredients is to do very little to them. That's what's going on here, with these rustic ingredients. Cut the steak into thin strips and add some guac and tomatoes to throw down some tasty taco action with the leftovers.

PREP TIME: **ABOUT 30 MINUTES, PLUS SOAKING AND MARINATING**
COOKING TIME: **ABOUT 1 HOUR**

BLACK BEANS

4 cups dried black beans

1 orange, halved

1 carrot, cut into 3 or 4 pieces

7 garlic cloves: 3 left whole, 4 thinly sliced

10 cilantro stems

3 fresh or dried bay leaves

3 sprigs fresh oregano

Salt

4 tablespoons (½ stick) unsalted butter

¼ cup vegetable oil

6 tomatillos, husks removed, diced

4 poblano chiles or other mild chiles (such as Anaheim), seeded and diced

1 white onion, diced

2 (12-ounce) cans cheap-ass beer

4 cups chicken stock, preferably homemade

2 sprigs epazote, optional (see page 156)

½ cup cilantro leaves

2 tablespoons fresh lime juice

STEAK AND CHIMICHURRI

5 garlic cloves

Salt

1 tablespoon extra-virgin olive oil

1 bunch flat-leaf parsley

½ bunch cilantro

½ cup fresh oregano leaves

¼ teaspoon red pepper flakes

¼ teaspoon smoked paprika

¼ cup red wine vinegar

Grated zest of 1 lemon

Grated zest of 1 lime

6 (6- to 8-ounce) skirt steaks

1 orange, halved

Freshly cracked black pepper

1. For the beans, soak them in enough cold water to cover by 1 or 2 inches for 8 to 10 hours or overnight. Change the water once or twice, if possible.

2. Drain the beans and transfer to a deep pot. Add 3 quarts of cold water and bring to a simmer over medium heat.

3. Meanwhile, spread a large double thickness of cheesecloth on a work surface and put the orange halves, carrot pieces, 3 whole garlic cloves, cilantro stems, bay leaves, and oregano in the center. Gather the cheesecloth together to make a sachet, or pouch. Tie it closed with kitchen twine and then drop the sachet into the simmering beans.

4. Simmer the beans for about 45 minutes, skimming off any foam that rises to the surface. When the beans are tender, season with salt, drain, and rinse them under cool water. Discard the sachet.

5. In a deep pot, heat the butter and vegetable oil. When the butter melts and both the oil and butter are hot, sauté the tomatillos, chiles, onion, and sliced garlic for about 2 minutes. Add the beer to deglaze the pot, scraping up any browned bits that stick to the bottom.

6. Add the stock and epazote. Bring to a simmer and add the beans. Cook for about 5 minutes, or until the beans are heated through and the stock is slightly reduced.

7. Fold in the cilantro and lime juice and season with salt.

8. For the steak and chimichurri, mash the garlic and a little salt using a mortar and pestle to make a paste. Add the olive oil and mash it into the paste.

9. Remove the leaves from the parsley and cilantro bunches and put the leaves in the mortar. Mash the leaves into the paste until it turns bright green. Add the oregano leaves and work in the mortar and pestle until smooth.

10. Transfer the chimichurri to a bowl. Fold the red pepper flakes and paprika into the chimichurri and then stir in the vinegar, lemon zest, and lime zest. Season with salt.

11. Spread about one-quarter of the chimichurri over the skirt steaks and put them in a dish large enough to hold them. Refrigerate the steaks for about 45 minutes.

12. Prepare a gas or charcoal grill so that the heating elements or coals are medium-hot.

13. Grill the orange halves, cut side down, for 3 to 4 minutes, or until the fruit softens and is lightly charred. Remove from the grill.

14. Season the steaks with salt and black pepper and grill for 3 to 4 minutes on each side for medium-rare, or to your desired degree of doneness. Let the steak rest.

15. Serve the steaks with a squeeze of juice from the charred orange halves and spoon some black beans next to the steaks. Pass the remaining chimichurri on the side.

Mexican Tea

Epazote is an herb that grows in Mexico and Latin America. It's also known as Mexican tea, wormseed, and *paico* and is frequently added to bean dishes, as it's credited with aiding digestion. Most folks who like Mexican food can't get enough of this distinctive herb, although I confess it can be an acquired taste. Younger, smaller leaves are milder than older, large leaves.

GRASS-FED, ORGANIC, AND NATURAL BEEF

Grass-fed beef is prized by home cooks and chefs alike, partly because it signifies a better life for the animal, and partly because it's leaner with a slightly beefier flavor than grain-fed beef. I don't own a ranch and I've never farmed, so I can only talk about what I've learned from others who are closer to the process than I am. Cattle that eat only grass and hay tend to spend their time in pastures, rather than feedlots. Because they are not fed grain, they gain weight a little more slowly and are slaughtered when they're a little older. Ask your butcher about grass-fed beef, or peruse the farmers' markets for it.

Some beef is also marketed as organic, which means the grass, hay, and any grains the cattle eat must be certified organic. The USDA's National Organic Program lays out the guidelines that farmers must follow before they can call their beef organic.

Finally, you can find natural beef, which simply means the animal was raised without growth hormones and antibiotics. These cattle might be grass-fed or might be fed grain in a feedlot.

Filet Mignon with Creamed Spinach and Watercress {SERVES 4}

CHICAGO, WHERE I LIVE, is known for great steak. Classic accompaniments such as creamed spinach, watercress, potatoes, and béarnaise sauce all make the steak's flavor shine and round out the meal. Now, filet mignon is excellent served this way, but it's pretty goddamn expensive, so it's fine to substitute a less pricey cut. You'll still mow down a tasty steak dish.

PREP TIME: **15 TO 20 MINUTES**
COOKING TIME: **45 TO 50 MINUTES**

CREAMED SPINACH AND WATERCRESS

6 tablespoons (¾ stick) unsalted butter

1 shallot, minced

¼ cup all-purpose flour

2 cups whole milk

1 cup heavy cream

Salt

2 ounces Gruyère cheese, grated (about ½ cup)

1 pound fresh spinach, stemmed

3 bunches watercress, thick stems removed

¼ teaspoon freshly grated nutmeg

Freshly cracked black pepper

FILET MIGNON

4 filets mignon (about 7 ounces each)

Coarse salt

Crushed peppercorns (I like to use Tellicherry peppercorns for their intense flavor)

¼ cup vegetable oil

6 ounces (1½ sticks) unsalted butter

4 garlic cloves

4 sprigs fresh thyme

1 sprig fresh rosemary

1. For the spinach and watercress, in a deep skillet, melt the butter over medium-high heat. When hot, cook the shallot for about 1 minute to soften. Whisk in the flour and cook for about 6 minutes, or until the flour and butter are fully mixed and take on the color of straw.

2. Add the milk and cream, season lightly with salt, and simmer, stirring occasionally, for about 20 minutes, until thick and creamy. Whisk in the cheese and cook until the cheese has completely melted. Cover to keep warm and set aside.

3. Bring a saucepan of salted water to a boil. Put a bowl of cold water and ice cubes near the stove. Add the spinach and watercress to the boiling water and blanch them for about 2 minutes, or until tender. Lift the greens from the boiling water and immediately plunge them into the ice bath.

4. Lift the greens from the ice bath and, using your hands or a dish towel, squeeze all the water from the greens. They should be as dry as possible.

5. Finely chop the spinach and watercress and then fold into the cream sauce.

6. Set the pot over medium heat and stir until the greens are fully incorporated and the sauce is heated through. Season with salt and pepper and serve, or cover to keep warm while the steak cooks.

7. For the filet mignon, preheat the oven to 400°F. Liberally season the steaks with salt and crushed pepper.

8. In a heavy, oven-safe skillet, heat the oil over high heat. When hot, sear the steaks in the hot pan for 3 minutes. Let a crust form on the steak by leaving it alone. Do not move it during this time. Flip the steaks and let them cook for 2 to 3 minutes longer. Again, do not move them in the pan but let them cook untouched so they develop a crust. Hey, don't even *look* at the steaks during this time.

9. Transfer the skillet to the oven and let the steaks cook for about 5 minutes. Return the skillet to the stovetop over medium-low heat. Add the butter, garlic, thyme, and rosemary and when the butter melts, baste the steaks with the sauce and cook for about 2 minutes longer for medium-rare.

10. Cover the skillet with a lid or tightly with aluminum foil and let the steaks rest in the pan for about 5 minutes.

11. Serve with the creamed spinach and watercress on the side.

Short Rib Stroganoff with Spaetzle, Wild Mushrooms, and Peppered Sour Cream {SERVES 6}

MOST OF MY COOKING is based on spontaneity, but this dish, which has become a signature of mine, is based on one of the few my mom had in her repertoire. I always loved it as a kid, and, as so many chefs before have done with recipes from their childhood, I tweaked it to suit my taste. I use short ribs instead of ground beef, and a peppery sour cream and wild mushroom sauce in place of the canned cream of mushroom soup Mom relied on.

PREP TIME: **ABOUT 45 MINUTES**
COOKING TIME: **ABOUT 4½ HOURS**

SHORT RIBS

1 tablespoon canola oil

5 pounds beef short ribs

1 tablespoon salt

1 tablespoon freshly ground black pepper

1 cup diced onions

½ cup diced carrots

½ cup diced celery

1 (750-ml) bottle Cabernet Sauvignon or similar red wine

8 cups beef stock, preferably homemade

2 garlic cloves

2 fresh bay leaves, or 1 dried

2 sprigs fresh thyme

1 teaspoon crushed star anise (1 to 2 stars)

1 teaspoon fennel seeds

MARMALADE

6 to 8 shallots, cut into rings about ⅛ inch thick (about 1 cup)

1 fresh bay leaf

1 allspice berry

1 whole clove

1 tablespoon sugar

¼ cup white wine vinegar

1 tablespoon sherry vinegar

½ teaspoon kosher salt

JUS

1 tablespoon plus 1½ teaspoons canola oil

1 large shallot, diced

1 garlic clove, minced

1 bay leaf

1 sprig fresh thyme

1 star anise

1 Thai peppercorn

1 cup Cabernet Sauvignon or similar red wine

PEPPERED SOUR CREAM

1 teaspoon whole pink peppercorns

1 teaspoon whole green peppercorns

2 teaspoons whole black peppercorns

2 cups sour cream

Salt

1 cup fresh dill sprigs, for garnish

Spaetzle (recipe follows)

Black Trumpet Mushrooms (recipe follows)

1. For the short ribs, preheat the oven to 250ºF.

2. In a heavy, oven-safe pot or Dutch oven, heat about half the oil over medium-high heat. Liberally season the ribs with salt and pepper. Sear on all sides until browned. As the ribs are browned, set aside, covered, until needed.

3. Add the rest of the oil to the pot and cook the onions, carrots, and celery for 3 to 4 minutes, or until lightly caramelized. Add the wine and stir gently to deglaze the pan, scraping the browned bits from the bottom of the pan.

4. Return the ribs to the pot and add the stock and 2 cups of water.

5. Put the garlic, bay leaves, thyme, star anise, and fennel seeds in a piece of cheesecloth. Gather the cheesecloth into a bundle and tie closed with a piece of kitchen twine to make a sachet. Add to the pot.

6. Cover the pot with its lid or tightly with aluminum foil and braise for about 4 hours, or until the meat is fork-tender. Add more stock or water, if necessary.

7. Lift the ribs from the pot and set aside to cool. Set the ribs on a rack sitting in a shallow pan to catch the drippings. Set aside the pot with the pan liquids.

8. Meanwhile, for the marmalade, put the shallots, bay leaf, allspice berry, clove, and sugar in a saucepan. Add the vinegars and 1 tablespoon of water. Bring to a simmer over medium heat. Cook for about 20 minutes, stirring occasionally, until the liquid nearly evaporates and the shallots are translucent and sticky. Season with salt.

9. Remove the allspice berry, clove, and bay leaf before serving.

10. For the jus, degrease the pan juices from cooking the ribs and strain them through a fine-mesh sieve. Discard the solids. Measure 2 cups of the pan juices.

11. In a saucepan, heat the oil over medium-high heat. Cook the shallot and garlic, stirring, until caramelized. Add the bay leaf, thyme, star anise, peppercorn, and wine. Bring the wine to a boil, reduce the heat, and simmer, scraping up the browned bits from the bottom of the pan. Add the 2 cups strained pan juices. Bring the sauce to a boil over medium-high heat. Reduce the heat and simmer a little more gently for about 2 hours, skimming any foam that rises to the surface. Adjust the heat up or down to maintain a simmer.

12. Strain the jus through a fine-mesh sieve three times until it is as clear as possible.

13. Carefully cut any fat from the cooled ribs and cut the meat into large cubes for serving.

14. For the peppered sour cream, in a large, dry skillet, toast the peppercorns over medium-high heat for about 3 minutes, or until aromatic.

15. Transfer the peppercorns to a spice grinder and grind finely. Fold the peppercorns into the sour cream and season with salt. Garnish with the dill.

16. To serve the short ribs, toss the cubed meat with the jus and serve it spooned over the spaetzle. Garnish the plate with the mushrooms, marmalade, and peppered sour cream.

Spaetzle {MAKES ABOUT 4 CUPS}

PREP TIME: **ABOUT 25 MINUTES**
COOKING TIME: **ABOUT 35 MINUTES**

1½ cups all-purpose flour

¾ cup sour cream

½ cup milk

3 large eggs

1 tablespoon stone-ground mustard

Salt and freshly ground black pepper

2 tablespoons unsalted butter

1 tablespoon chopped fresh chives

1. In a large bowl, whisk the flour, sour cream, and milk until smooth. Add the eggs and mustard and stir until smooth. Season to taste with salt and pepper. Set aside to rest for 20 minutes.

2. Bring a large pot of water to a boil. Reduce the heat so the water simmers. Using a spaetzle machine or perforated pan, drop the batter in small amounts into the simmering water. When the spaetzle rise to the surface of the water, simmer for 1 minute and then remove from the water with a slotted spoon.

3. In a sauté pan, melt the butter over medium-high heat. When hot, cook the spaetzle for about 5 minutes, or until the edges turn golden. Season with the chives and salt and serve hot.

Black Trumpet Mushrooms {MAKES ABOUT 4 CUPS}

PREP TIME: **ABOUT 10 MINUTES**
COOKING TIME: **ABOUT 10 MINUTES**

12 ounces (3 sticks) unsalted butter

6 shallots, minced (about 1 cup)

2 pounds black trumpet mushrooms or other mushrooms (foraged are full flavored), left whole

½ cup mushroom stock or water

¼ cup sherry vinegar

2 tablespoons grapeseed oil

Salt and freshly ground black pepper

1. In a large sauté pan, melt the butter over medium-high heat. Add the shallots and mushrooms and cook for about 10 minutes, or until the mushrooms soften.

2. Transfer one-third of the mushrooms and shallots to a blender. Add the stock, vinegar, and oil and blend until smooth.

3. Strain the sauce through a fine-mesh sieve. Season with salt and pepper. Serve hot.

4. Use the rest of the mushrooms to garnish the Stroganoff.

Mom's Brisket Pot Roast {SERVES 6}

I'M TOTALLY A LYING BASTARD for calling this Mom's Brisket Pot Roast. Pretty sure my mom couldn't pick a brisket out of a lineup. Mom makes a pretty good pot roast, but it's my wife, Allie, who is the *MasterChef* of the slow cooker. And we all know a slow cooker (or Crock-Pot) is the pot roast's best friend—although I don't use one here. The fun part of making this is deciding which veggies you want to use. In the summer, lighten the dish with tomatoes, summer squash, zucchini, and basil, and in the cold weather, go the classic root vegetable route.

PREP TIME: **ABOUT 30 MINUTES, PLUS RESTING**
COOKING TIME: **3½ TO 4 HOURS**

BRISKET

- 1 (6- to 7-pound) center-cut brisket, fat cap scored but not removed
- Coarse salt and coarsely ground black pepper
- 6 garlic cloves, smashed
- 2 tablespoons fresh thyme leaves
- 1 tablespoon red pepper flakes
- 1 tablespoon piment d'Espelette, cayenne pepper, or hot paprika
- 4 fresh bay leaves
- 6 tablespoons vegetable oil
- 3 carrots, peeled and cut into large dice
- 2 yellow or white onions, cut into large dice
- 2 celery stalks, cut into large dice
- 1 leek, white and light green parts only, cut into large dice
- 2 anchovy fillets (optional)
- 1½ teaspoons tomato paste
- 2 cups good red wine
- 4 cups beef stock (preferably homemade), plus more as needed

VEGETABLE GARNISH

- ½ cup olive oil
- 3 parsnips, peeled and cut into large dice
- 3 purple carrots, peeled and cut into large dice
- 1 small red onion, cut into large dice
- 1 watermelon radish, peeled and cut into large dice (see Note)
- 1 bunch hakurei turnips (6 or 7 turnips), peeled and quartered (see Note)
- Kosher salt

1. For the brisket, remove the brisket from the refrigerator about 1½ hours before preparing. Rub it liberally with salt and pepper. Rub the garlic over the meat, along with the thyme, red pepper flakes, and piment d'Espelette. Toss the bay leaves on top of the brisket.

2. Preheat the oven to 325°F.

3. In a heavy roasting pan set over two burners, heat the vegetable oil over high heat. When it shimmers, sear the brisket, fat side down, for 6 to 8 minutes on each side. Remove the brisket from the pan and set aside. (You can use a Dutch oven.)

4. Put the carrots, onions, celery, and leek in the roasting pan and cook for about 8 minutes, scraping the bottom of the pan with a wooden spoon to loosen any browned bits sticking to the pan. When the vegetables begin to caramelize, add the anchovies, if using, and tomato paste and cook, stirring, until the tomato paste looks rusty in color.

5. Add the wine, continuing to scrape the bottom of the pan to release any crispy bits. Add the stock and bring to a simmer.

6. Return the brisket to the roasting pan. If there is not enough liquid to cover the meat, add more stock or water so that it is barely covered. Cover tightly with aluminum foil and put the roasting pan in the oven. Roast for 3½ to 4 hours, or until the meat is fork-tender.

7. For the vegetable garnish, increase the oven temperature to 350°F. (If you have two ovens, use them both—one for the brisket and the other for the veg.)

8. In a roasting pan set over two burners, heat the olive oil over medium-high heat. When hot, add the vegetables and roll to coat them in the oil. Season with about 1 teaspoon of salt.

9. Transfer the roasting pan to the oven and roast for 20 to 25 minutes, or until the vegetables are tender and lightly caramelized.

10. Transfer the brisket to a cutting board, tent with foil, and let it rest for about 10 minutes before carving.

11. Strain the pan juices through a fine-mesh sieve into a large saucepan. Discard the vegetables that cooked alongside the brisket. Skim the fat from the pan juices. Bring the pan juices to a simmer over medium heat and cook for 10 to 12 minutes, until reduced by half.

12. Slice the brisket against the grain. Arrange the slices on a serving platter and spoon the braising liquid over the meat. Arrange the vegetable garnish around the meat and serve.

NOTE: Watermelon radishes earned their name because when cut open, their beautiful pink interior surrounded by a green-and-white exterior resembles summer's juiciest melon. These radishes are sweet and mild compared to run-of-the-mill red radishes, and regularly measure about 3 inches in diameter. They can be roasted, as I do in this recipe, and also are wonderful eaten raw. Some home cooks and gardeners like to pickle them. They are also called red heart radishes.

Hakurei turnips are sweet, small, and smooth, measuring only about 2 inches in diameter. They can be eaten raw but usually are cooked. If you can't find these delicious little turnips, substitute small common turnips.

Pork Chops with Sweet Potato Latkes and Cinnamon-Spiced Apples {SERVES 4}

PORK IS EATEN PRETTY much everywhere in the world, but something about pork chops says all-American. I decided to add some texture to the dish with little potato pancakes called latkes, first cousins to hash browns. Cinnamon-spiced apples, flavored with both apple cider and beer, brighten up the plate and happily carry this from summer's backyard to the cooler days of fall. Heck, this would work well for breakfast, too—just add a fried egg or two to the plate.

PREP TIME: **ABOUT 30 MINUTES, PLUS CHILLING**
COOKING TIME: **40 TO 42 MINUTES**

PORK CHOPS

- 1 cup kosher salt
- ½ cup sugar
- 6 whole black peppercorns
- 6 coriander seeds
- 3 cardamom pods
- 2 fresh bay leaves
- 1 black tea bag
- 4 (10- to 12-ounce) pork chops (I use Berkshire pork)

CINNAMON-SPICED APPLES

- 2 Honeycrisp or Jonagold apples
- 2 tablespoons unsalted butter
- 1 Ceylon cinnamon stick
- ½ cup German lager
- ½ cup hard apple cider
- Salt

SWEET POTATO LATKES

- 2 pounds sweet potatoes, peeled
- 1 small onion
- 2 teaspoons kosher salt
- 3 large eggs, whisked
- ¼ cup sliced scallions (3 to 4 scallions)
- 3 tablespoons all-purpose flour
- Vegetable oil, for frying
- Coarse sea salt and coarsely cracked black pepper

1. For the pork chops, in a large pot, mix the salt, sugar, peppercorns, coriander seeds, cardamom pods, bay leaves, and the tea bag. Add about 8 cups of water and bring to a brisk simmer over medium-high heat. Remove from the heat and strain the brine through a fine-mesh sieve. Discard the solids. Let the brine cool.

2. Put the pork chops in a dish or pan large enough to hold them in a single layer. Pour the brine over the chops, cover, and refrigerate for 8 hours or overnight. Rinse the brine off the chops and pat them dry with paper towels. Let them sit at room temperature to get the chill off while you prepare the grill and make the apples and latkes.

3. For the cinnamon-spiced apples, peel and core the apples. Cut them into thin wedges.

4. In a large skillet, heat the butter and cinnamon stick over medium heat. When the butter has melted, add the apple wedges and cook for about 5 minutes, until browned.

5. Add the lager and cider and cook over medium heat for about 5 minutes, until the apples are glazed and most of the liquid evaporates. Season the apples with salt and cover to keep hot.

6. Prepare a charcoal or gas grill so that the coals or heating elements are medium-hot. Grill the chops for 6 minutes on each side, or until cooked to the desired doneness. Set aside to rest while you make the latkes.

7. For the sweet potato latkes, using a box grater, grate the sweet potatoes and onion. Transfer to a large bowl and toss with the salt. Fold in the eggs and scallions. Sprinkle the flour over the potato mixture and, using your hands, mix gently but thoroughly.

8. Pour oil into a large skillet to a depth of about 1 inch. Heat over medium-high heat until the oil is hot and shimmering and registers 350° to 360°F on a deep-fry thermometer.

9. Pinch off a large spoonful of the potato mixture and squeeze any excess liquid from it with your fingers. Carefully lower the amount into the hot oil and fry for about 5 minutes, or until golden brown. With a long-handled spoon or tongs, turn the latke in the oil. You should be able to cook about 5 latkes at once in the skillet. As they cook, lift the latkes from the oil with a slotted spoon and drain them on a paper towel–lined tray.

10. Season the pork with coarse salt and pepper and serve with the latkes and apples.

Roasted Goat with Salsa Verde and Grilled Onions {SERVES 4}

SO, GOAT MAY SEEM CRAZY, but it's actually the most cooked meat on earth! As delicious as this goat is, it's also super simple—the easy brine makes the goat juicier than ever. (And if you can't get goat, make this with pork chops instead.) If you've never cooked goat, give it a try. Like lamb, it can be served rare or well done. Up to you.

I usually serve this in the summer because of the easy access to fresh herbs—which you can mix and match any way you want. Typically, salsa verde is made primarily with parsley but I stray from that dictate by adding a number of other fresh herbs. Teamed with the goat, the salsa makes this just the thing for those hot, humid months. So, fire up the grill and get cookin'.

PREP TIME: **ABOUT 20 MINUTES, PLUS CHILLING**
COOKING TIME: **25 TO 30 MINUTES**

BRINE AND GOAT

- 1 cup salt
- ½ cup sugar
- 1 black tea bag
- 6 whole black peppercorns
- 6 coriander seeds
- 3 cardamom pods
- 2 fresh bay leaves
- 4 (10- to 12-ounce) goat chops

SALSA VERDE

- 1 cup flat-leaf parsley leaves
- ¾ cup cilantro leaves
- ½ cup mint leaves
- ¼ cup fresh tarragon leaves
- ¼ cup fresh lemon balm leaves (see Note)
- 1 cup extra-virgin olive oil
- 2 garlic cloves, thinly sliced
- 1 shallot, minced
- 1 tablespoon grated lemon zest
- 1 tablespoon grated lime zest
- ¼ teaspoon red pepper flakes
- Coarse sea salt and freshly ground black pepper

GRILLED ONIONS

- 1 bunch torpedo onions, shallots, or small red onions (about 8 small onions)
- Olive oil
- Salt and freshly ground black pepper
- 1 teaspoon fresh lemon juice

1. For the brine and goat, put 8 cups of water in a large pot and add the salt, sugar, tea bag, peppercorns, coriander seeds, cardamom pods, and bay leaves. Bring to a simmer over medium-low heat and simmer for about 15 minutes.

2. Strain the brine through a fine-mesh sieve into a bowl. Discard the solids and allow the brine to cool.

3. Put the goat chops in the cooled brine, making sure the meat is covered. Cover and refrigerate for at least 8 hours or overnight.

4. Lift the goat from the brine and pat dry with paper towels.

5. For the salsa verde, coarsely chop the parsley, cilantro, mint, tarragon, and lemon balm and place them in a bowl. Add the extra-virgin olive oil and stir in the garlic, shallot, lemon zest, lime zest, and red pepper flakes. Season with salt and pepper.

6. Prepare a charcoal or gas grill so that the coals or heating elements are medium-hot, or use a stovetop grill pan. Grill the goat for 6 minutes on each side, or until cooked to the desired doneness. Keep the grill or grill pan hot.

7. For the grilled onions, trim off the root ends. Split the onions in half and drizzle with olive oil. Season with salt and pepper.

8. Put the onions on the grill or hot grill pan and cook for about 1 minute on each side, or until the onions begin to blister and soften. Remove the onions from the grill and sprinkle the lemon juice over them.

9. Put a chop on each of four serving plates. Slather with the salsa verde and then gingerly lay 1 or 2 onions on the plates or over the chops and serve.

NOTE: Lemon balm is light and lemony but not easy to find. The best bet is to grow it yourself. If you don't have a green thumb and can't find lemon balm in the farmers' market, increase the quantity of another herb listed here, such as parsley or a mixture of mint and tarragon.

Yogurt-Marinated Leg of Lamb with Crushed Olive Oil Potatoes and Grainy Mustard {SERVES 4}

BOTH LAMB AND YOGURT show up on Mediterranean menus, and for good reason. Yogurt's acidic tang breaks down some of the tougher leg muscles during marinating, and at the same time tempers some of the meat's natural gaminess. The crushed potatoes doused with olive oil and seasoned with rosemary add body to the dish without reliance on heavier cream and butter.

PREP TIME: **ABOUT 20 MINUTES, PLUS MARINATING AND RESTING**
COOKING TIME: **36 TO 38 MINUTES**

4 cups plain yogurt

6 garlic cloves, crushed

Grated zest of 1 lemon

1 tablespoon whole black peppercorns, toasted (see Note)

1 (2-pound) boneless leg of lamb

4 cups beef stock, preferably homemade

½ cup whole-grain mustard

1 tablespoon honey

Salt

1 pound small and medium Yukon Gold potatoes, halved if large

½ cup olive oil

Leaves from 2 sprigs fresh rosemary

Freshly ground black pepper

1. In a medium bowl, whisk the yogurt, garlic, lemon zest, and peppercorns. Put the lamb in a dish large enough to hold it and pour the marinade over the meat. Turn it a few times to ensure it's coated. Cover and refrigerate for 8 hours or overnight.

2. In a saucepan, bring the beef stock to a boil. Cook for 8 to 10 minutes, or until reduced to about 1 cup. Stir in the mustard and honey. Cover to keep warm and set aside.

3. Bring a large saucepan filled with lightly salted water to a boil. Add the potatoes and cook for about 20 minutes, or until tender. Drain the potatoes and put them in a shallow bowl. Using a fork, crush the potatoes. Add the oil and rosemary leaves. Season with salt and pepper. Cover to keep warm.

4. Prepare a charcoal or gas grill so that the coals or heating elements are hot.

5. Lift the lamb from the marinade and let the marinade drip off the meat. Grill the lamb for about 4 minutes on each side or until cooked to the desired degree of doneness. Let the lamb rest for about 15 minutes and then slice.

6. Divide the potatoes among four serving plates. Top the potatoes with slices of lamb and drizzle with the mustard sauce.

NOTE: To toast the peppercorns, spread them in a dry pan and toast over medium-high heat for 3 to 5 minutes, until aromatic.

6
A WALK THROUGH the GARDEN

Kale with Roasted Beets,
Goat Cheese, and Pine Nuts

Haricots Verts Casserole
with Crispy Shallots
and Wild Mushrooms

Pureed Butternut Squash

Fingerling Potato Confit

Brussels Sprout Hash
with Apples, Smoked Bacon,
and Walnuts

Ginger-Glazed Carrots

Braised Cabbage with Caraway

French Lentils with Pearl Onions

Fennel Ratatouille

Sautéed Rapini
with Toasted Garlic

Refried Cannellini Beans
with Saffron and Garlic

Grilled Asparagus
with Smoked Béarnaise

Maple Whipped Yams

I'M GONNA BE HONEST with you: I suck at gardening. I've tried to grow my own tomatoes, cucumbers, melons, and herbs and all of them end up the same way—shriveled and brown, infested with bugs, and listlessly lying on the ground. The few times they actually look like they're doing okay, they become lunch for the damn squirrels and rabbits that party outside my house.

All this makes me more in awe of the men and women who grow and pick the amazing fruits and veggies I rely on both at home and in the restaurant. I like to source ingredients that speak of the season at hand, and for the most part that means shopping at the local farmers' market. It's all about working with vegetables that farmers put as much love into growing as I'll put into cooking.

Not everybody has the same access to these products or the budget to afford them, so just try to get things that are as fresh as possible and cook 'em as quickly as you can so that they're still at their peak.

Kale with Roasted Beets, Goat Cheese, and Pine Nuts {SERVES 6}

THE OUTCOME OF THIS SIMPLE DISH depends solely on the quality of the ingredients—nothing fancy going on here. All the flavors go together splendidly, so it's hard to screw this up if you hit the farmers' market and buy odd, ugly, gnarled beets and a few varieties of kale. These less-than-perfect veggies tend to have lots of personality, which, for a veg, equals great flavor.

PREP TIME: **ABOUT 15 MINUTES**
COOKING TIME: **55 TO 70 MINUTES**

3 beets

3 garlic cloves, plus 2 teaspoons chopped garlic

1 tablespoon whole black peppercorns

½ cup pine nuts

1 bunch kale

2 tablespoons plus 2 teaspoons fresh lemon juice

Salt and freshly ground pepper

2 tablespoons olive oil

1 (2-ounce) log goat cheese, crumbled

1. Preheat the oven to 400ºF.

2. Put the beets, garlic cloves, and peppercorns in a small roasting pan. Add enough water to come a third of the way up the beets. Cover with aluminum foil and bake for 45 to 60 minutes, or until the beets are still firm but are tender enough to have a little give when pressed.

3. Remove the beets from the roasting pan and let them cool a little. Do not turn off the oven.

4. Holding the beets in a kitchen towel, slip the skins from the beets. They should slide off easily.

5. Let the beets cool a little more and slice each into 8 slices (or thereabouts). Put the slices in a large bowl.

6. Spread the pine nuts in a single layer in a small baking pan and toast in the oven for 7 to 10 minutes, or until lightly browned. Rotate the pan halfway through cooking and stir the pine nuts once or twice to ensure even cooking. Transfer the pine nuts to a plate to stop the cooking and then add them to the bowl with the beets.

7. Remove and discard any tough outer leaves from the kale and then pull the rest of the leaves from the stems; discard the stems. Wash the leaves under cool, running water and divide them into 4 batches, which will make cooking easier. Coarsely chop the kale.

8. Set a large, dry sauté pan over medium-high heat. When very hot, sauté the first batch of kale for about 30 seconds. Some of the leaves will brown, which is a good thing. Add ½ teaspoon of the chopped garlic and sauté the kale and garlic for about 30 seconds longer. Finally, add 2 teaspoons of the lemon juice and season with salt and pepper. Lift the kale from the pan and add it to the bowl with the beets. Continue cooking the remaining three batches in the same way and add them to the bowl with the beets.

9. Toss the beets, pine nuts, and kale and drizzle with oil. Add the cheese and serve.

Haricots Verts Casserole with Crispy Shallots and Wild Mushrooms

{SERVES 6 TO 8 GENEROUSLY}

THIS IS BASED ON CAMPBELL'S famous green bean casserole, which annually finds its way to Thanksgiving tables across the country. I like to reinvent classics, and here I switch out the onions for shallots and make a wild mushroom béchamel in place of the can of cream of mushroom soup. When you fry the shallots, make sure the oil's temp is perfect. The little onions are very thin, and because they have more sugar than other onions, they fry up lickety-split. Keep an eye on 'em.

PREP TIME: **30 TO 35 MINUTES**
COOKING TIME: **40 TO 45 MINUTES**

MUSHROOM BÉCHAMEL

8 ounces chanterelle mushrooms, stemmed and quartered

½ cup olive oil

Salt and freshly ground black pepper

8 tablespoons (1 stick) unsalted butter

¼ cup chopped onions

¼ cup all-purpose flour

8 cups whole milk

¼ teaspoon freshly grated nutmeg

2 fresh bay leaves (optional)

SAUTÉED WILD MUSHROOMS

8 tablespoons (1 stick) unsalted butter

1 garlic clove, minced

2 sprigs fresh thyme

8 ounces wild mushrooms

¼ cup sherry vinegar

Salt and freshly ground black pepper

SHALLOTS AND HARICOTS VERTS

4 cups vegetable oil

Salt

3 cups thinly sliced shallots (about 8 ounces)

2 pounds haricots verts

1. For the mushroom béchamel, preheat the oven to 375ºF.

2. Rub the mushrooms with 6 tablespoons of the olive oil and spread them on a baking sheet or in a shallow baking pan. Season lightly with salt and pepper and roast for 12 to 15 minutes, or until lightly browned and tender. Remove and let cool.

3. When the mushrooms are cool enough to handle, coarsely chop them and transfer to a blender. Add a little water and the remaining 2 tablespoons of olive oil and puree until smooth. Set aside.

4. In a saucepan, cook the butter and onions over medium heat until the butter melts and the onions are translucent. Add the flour and stir with a wooden spoon until the béchamel pulls away from the sides of the pan. While stirring, gradually add the milk, stirring to combine. Add the nutmeg and bay leaves, if using, and let the sauce cook for about 15 minutes, or until the béchamel is heated through and any raw flour flavor is gone. Fold the pureed mushrooms into the sauce. Strain the sauce through a sieve into a bowl, cover, and set aside until needed.

5. For the sautéed wild mushrooms, in a sauté pan, melt the butter over medium heat and add the garlic and thyme. When the butter begins to bubble, add the mushrooms and cook, stirring, for about 3 minutes, or until the mushrooms are cooked through and softened, but not mushy.

6. Remove the pan from the heat and toss the mushrooms with the vinegar. Season to taste with salt and pepper and then transfer the mushrooms to a paper towel–lined plate.

7. For the shallots and haricots verts, put the vegetable oil in a large pot and heat over high heat until it registers 350ºF on a deep-fry thermometer. Separately, bring a large pot of heavily salted water to a boil. It should be salted enough so that it tastes like the ocean. Set a large metal bowl filled with ice and cold water near the stove.

8. Carefully submerge the shallots in the hot oil and fry for about 90 seconds, until golden brown. Using a slotted spoon, lift the shallots from the oil and drain on paper towels. Season lightly with salt.

9. Drop a handful of the beans in the boiling water and blanch for 30 seconds. Lift the beans from the boiling water and immediately submerge in the ice bath to cool. Work in batches, letting the water return to a boil between each batch.

10. Fold the beans and mushrooms into the béchamel. Warm over medium-low heat until heated through. Spoon into a serving bowl and garnish with the fried shallots.

WILD MUSHROOMS

The term "wild mushrooms" covers a lot of territory. Few are actually gathered in the wild anymore, as mushroom growers have turned their attention to cultivating the earthy and delicious fungi. When buying the mushrooms for a recipe that calls for "wild" or "forest" mushrooms, look for *any* mushrooms that appear firm, dry, and plump. This is more important than the specific type. In most cases, one can be substituted for another with tasty results. And if you experience sticker shock, buy fewer wild mushrooms than called for and make up the difference with ordinary mushrooms.

The mushrooms will have names such as chanterelle, oyster, porcini, and shiitake. If you strike out at the market when looking for wild mushrooms, use cremini or white button mushrooms. The flavor won't be as deep and rich, but it will still be good.

Pureed Butternut Squash {SERVES 6}

THIS SIDE DISH EXEMPLIFIES "cooking in the season." It's totally down to earth and yet, above all else, celebrates the flavor and texture of the squash. Autumn falls between the lush bounty of summer and the slim pickins of winter, and one of its many blessings is the cool array of squashes. Butternut is an all-time favorite and for this dish, you can process the cooked squash so that it's chunky and rustic, or puree the daylights out of it and serve it as an elegant, velvety bisque.

PREP TIME: **6 TO 8 MINUTES**
COOKING TIME: **ABOUT 45 MINUTES**

1 butternut squash

8 tablespoons (1 stick) unsalted butter

2 tablespoons brown sugar

1 tablespoon maple syrup

1 tablespoon salt

1. Preheat the oven to 400°F.

2. Cut the squash in half lengthwise and scoop out the seeds. Put the two halves, flesh sides up, in a deep, rimmed roasting pan.

3. Dot the squash with about half the butter and sprinkle with the brown sugar. Season lightly with salt.

4. Add enough water to the pan to come about a third of the way up the sides of the squash. Cover with aluminum foil and bake for about 45 minutes, or until the squash is tender when pierced with a fork or small knife.

5. Remove the pan from the oven and transfer the squash halves to a work surface. Using a spoon, scrape the flesh from the squash and put it in the canister of a blender. Discard the squash skin. Add the maple syrup, the rest of the butter, and the salt and blend on low speed until the puree starts to come together. Increase the speed and blend for about 3 minutes, or until the squash is smooth. Taste and adjust the seasonings. Reheat over medium-low heat, if needed. Serve hot.

Fingerling Potato Confit {SERVES 6}

THERE ARE FEW WORDS in the cooking lexicon as sexy as "duck fat." It's been used to preserve food for hundreds of years, resulting in what the French call confit. When you cook something very slowly in fat—in this recipe, potatoes—the fat penetrates the food and infuses it with the rich, heady essence of the fat's intrinsic duck flavor. The method ensures that the food will last a lot longer than if it were cooked in liquid, and let's face it, nothing compares when it comes to flavor. Of course, if you would rather not use a quart (or more) of duck fat, use oil. I suggest olive oil, walnut oil, hazelnut oil, or your favorite. Go forth and get crazy.

PREP TIME: 18 TO 20 MINUTES
COOKING TIME: ABOUT 1 HOUR 40 MINUTES

1 quart duck fat	1 bunch fresh thyme
1 whole head garlic	2 tablespoons coarse sea salt
1½ pounds fingerling potatoes	

1. Preheat the oven to 250°F.

2. Put the duck fat in a baking dish large enough to hold the potatoes in a single layer and warm in the oven until the fat is fluid.

3. Peel the papery outer skin from the head of garlic and slice off the end. With a large knife, slice lengthwise through the cloves.

4. Make sure the potatoes are dry and then submerge them in the duck fat. Add the sliced garlic and thyme, cover with aluminum foil, and bake for 1½ hours, or until the potatoes are tender when pierced with a fork.

5. Lift the potatoes from the duck fat and transfer to a serving platter. Scatter the salt over them and serve hot.

6. Strain the duck fat through a fine-mesh sieve, cover, and refrigerate for up to 2 weeks. Use it again to confit more potatoes or something else.

Brussels Sprout Hash with Apples, Smoked Bacon, and Walnuts {SERVES 6 TO 8}

I'VE HAD THIS DISH on the menu for as long as I can remember, and always during the winter holidays from November to January. I love the distinct flavor of the walnuts, although you can use pecans with similar results. I call this "hash" as a way to describe a dish in which a few things cook together until they form a collective mixture.

PREP TIME: **ABOUT 12 MINUTES**
COOKING TIME: **16 TO 18 MINUTES**

4 pounds brussels sprouts, tough outer leaves removed and stems trimmed

Juice of 1 lemon

4 Granny Smith or other firm, tart apples

1 pound unsliced smoked bacon

1 onion, diced

Salt

2 tablespoons apple cider vinegar

Leaves from 2 sprigs fresh rosemary, minced

Freshly ground black pepper

1 cup coarsely chopped toasted walnuts (see Note)

1. Coarsely chop the brussels sprouts and set aside.

2. Stir the lemon juice into a bowl of cold water. Core and dice the apples (no reason to peel them unless you want to) and put them in the acidulated water to keep them from turning brown.

3. Dice the bacon and sauté over medium-high heat in a large skillet. When the bacon begins to brown, add the onion and cook for 10 to 12 minutes, until the onion softens and the bacon is browned. Set the skillet aside.

4. Bring a large pot of heavily salted water to a boil. It should be salted enough so that it tastes like the ocean. Set a large metal bowl filled with ice cubes and cold water near the stove. Drop the brussels sprouts into the boiling water and blanch for 2 minutes. Using a slotted spoon, lift the sprouts from the water and plunge them into the ice bath to cool. Drain the sprouts and transfer them to the skillet with the bacon and onion.

5. Drain the apples and add them to the skillet. Cook, stirring, for about 4 minutes, or until the brussels sprouts and apples are tender.

6. Add the vinegar and rosemary and season with salt and pepper. Top with the walnuts and serve.

NOTE: To toast the walnuts, spread them on a baking sheet and roast them in a 350°F oven for about 10 minutes, or until they darken a shade and are aromatic. Transfer to a plate to cool before coarsely chopping.

Ginger-Glazed Carrots {SERVES 6}

CARROTS ARE TOTALLY OVERLOOKED these days, too often relegated to simmering stockpots or kids' lunchboxes. Here, they are the rightful star on the plate. The aromatic spices provide depth and a delicious perfume to the dish, but it's the butter and honey that make it sing. Cook these guys slow and low and you'll be in good shape.

PREP TIME: **ABOUT 10 MINUTES**
COOKING TIME: **20 TO 22 MINUTES**

1½ pounds red, white, and orange carrots, with green tops

1 teaspoon ground green cardamom (see Note)

1 tablespoon coriander seeds

8 ounces (2 sticks) unsalted butter

1 nub fresh ginger, peeled

4 cups carrot juice

1 cup honey

Salt and freshly ground black pepper

1. Peel the carrots and cut them into 1-inch pieces (or larger if you prefer). Chop the green carrot tops. Set aside.

2. In a dry medium sauté pan, toast the cardamom and coriander seeds over medium heat for about 2 minutes, or until lightly browned and fragrant.

3. Add the butter and let it melt. Add the carrots and stir to combine.

4. With the back of a large knife, crush the ginger and add it to the pan. Add the carrot juice and honey and cook over low heat, covered, for about 20 minutes, or until the carrots are tender and nicely glazed. Stir several times during cooking to coat the carrots with the pan sauces. Most of the liquid will evaporate.

5. Remove the ginger from the pan and add the carrot tops. Season with salt and pepper, stir well, and serve.

NOTE: Cardamom is sold either in pods (husks) or as seeds, which have been removed from the pod. Before using the seeds, toast them in a dry skillet over medium heat for a few minutes, or until fragrant and slightly darkened. Let the seeds cool and then grind them in a spice grinder or coffee grinder.

The Juices Have It I love a good carrot or apple juice at a juice bar, but the only way to duplicate these at home is with a juice extractor. This powerful machine separates the juice of a fruit or veg from the fiber for a crazy-intense drink that tastes even *more* like the original. Carrot juice is very carrot-y; apple juice is very apple-y. Mix the two together and you have an awesome treat.

As delicious as the juices are, juice extractors are relatively expensive. They also require careful and somewhat tedious cleaning and might not be for everybody. Which brings me to another point. When I ask you to use carrot juice, you can probably buy it at the local natural food store or health bar. It doesn't keep well, so try to buy it on the day you're using it.

Braised Cabbage with Caraway {SERVES 6}

CABBAGE AND CARAWAY ARE BFFS, and rightfully so. Together they make a formidable team of flavor and texture, particularly when the caraway is properly toasted, a step that releases its natural oils and concentrates its flavor and aroma. This little dish has ties to eastern and central Europe and is as far from ostentatious as it could possibly be. Nothing fancy, just great flavor.

PREP TIME: **ABOUT 10 MINUTES**
COOKING TIME: **40 TO 45 MINUTES**

8 ounces (2 sticks) unsalted butter

2 tablespoons caraway seeds

1 Spanish onion, diced

2 heads savoy or napa cabbage, shaved or shredded

Leaves from 6 sprigs fresh thyme, chopped

4 cups vegetable stock, preferably homemade

Salt and freshly ground black pepper

1. Melt the butter in a large roasting pan or skillet over medium-high heat. Spread the caraway seeds in the pan and roast for 3 to 5 minutes, or until lightly browned and nutty smelling. Add the onion and cook for about 10 minutes, or until translucent.

2. Add the cabbage, thyme, and stock to the pan, season with salt and pepper, and bring to a simmer. Cook for about 30 minutes, until the cabbage is wilted and tender. Adjust the heat up or down to maintain a simmer. Serve hot.

French Lentils with Pearl Onions

{SERVES 4 TO 6}

I SUPPOSE IT'S NOT SURPRISING that the French perfected the art of cooking legumes (a fancy word for plants with seeds that grow in pods, i.e., beans and peas). Lentils are one of their triumphs and are one of my favorites, too, partly because they don't require long soaking but mostly because they taste so good. Lentils like to surround themselves with pearl onions, bacon, and thyme. At the restaurant we serve this dish alongside simple roasted chicken, although it could easily work with pork or beef. Let it cool down and serve it as a salad, too.

PREP TIME: **ABOUT 10 MINUTES**
COOKING TIME: **28 TO 32 MINUTES**

½ cup olive oil

4 tablespoons (½ stick) unsalted butter

1 pound pearl onions, peeled

3 carrots, peeled and diced

1 fennel bulb, cored and diced

3 garlic cloves, thinly sliced

Salt

2 cups Puy lentils

2 fresh bay leaves

1½ teaspoons chopped fresh thyme leaves

4 cups chicken stock, preferably homemade

1 tablespoon chopped flat-leaf parsley

1½ teaspoons minced fresh chives

1½ teaspoons chopped fresh tarragon

Fresh lemon juice

Freshly ground black pepper

1. In a Dutch oven or deep casserole dish, heat the oil and butter over medium-high heat. When hot, cook the onions, carrots, fennel, and garlic, stirring, for 3 to 4 minutes, or until the vegetables start to soften. Season with a pinch of salt.

2. Add the lentils, bay leaves, and thyme and toast, stirring, for about 30 seconds to coat the lentils evenly with the oil and butter. Add the stock and 2 cups of water to the pot and bring to a boil. Reduce the heat and simmer for 25 to 28 minutes, or until the lentils are tender but not mushy. Remove and discard the bay leaves.

3. Fold in the parsley, chives, and tarragon. Season with lemon juice, salt, and pepper. Serve right away.

Fennel Ratatouille {SERVES 6}

RATATOUILLE IS AS FUN to make as it is to say! There's a lot of knife work to prep it, but once you get past the chopping and dicing, the veggies just simmer away in the pan, making this easy breezy. Most recipes for this beloved side don't include fennel, but since I love its licorice-anise flavor, I throw it in. If you like its flavor as much as I do, chop up the feathery green fronds that top the bulb and toss them into the ratatouille at the end of the cooking—any earlier and you'll destroy their delicate flavor.

PREP TIME: **ABOUT 15 MINUTES, PLUS STANDING**
COOKING TIME: **ABOUT 55 MINUTES**

2 medium zucchini, chopped

2 medium yellow summer squash, sliced

1 medium eggplant, seeded and chopped

Salt

½ cup olive oil

1 Spanish onion, sliced

4 garlic cloves, minced

2 fennel bulbs, cored, trimmed and diced

8 Roma (plum) tomatoes, peeled, quartered, and seeded

8 ounces canned tomatoes (I use San Marzano tomatoes), drained

Freshly ground black pepper

Leaves from 6 sprigs fresh oregano, chopped

2 tablespoons chopped fresh basil

1. Mix the zucchini, summer squash, and eggplant in a large bowl. Sprinkle generously with salt and set aside to give the salt time to draw out moisture. (I generally do this overnight and rinse the vegetables in the morning, wringing the eggplant out like a towel. The salt removes moisture from the vegetables' cells by breaking them down so they are less apt to absorb liquid and turn soggy.)

2. In a large sauté pan, heat the oil over medium-high heat. When hot, cook the onion and garlic for about 10 minutes, or until the onion is translucent.

3. Put the salted vegetables in a colander and rinse under cool running water. Discard the liquid in the bowl.

4. Add the fennel and rinsed vegetables to the pan and cook, stirring, until heated through. Add the fresh and canned tomatoes, bring to a simmer, and cook for about 45 minutes, or until thickened to a stewlike consistency. Raise or lower the heat to maintain a simmer.

5. Season with salt and pepper and serve in bowls, topped with the oregano and basil.

Sautéed Rapini with Toasted Garlic

{SERVES 6}

RAPINI, ALSO CALLED BROCCOLI RABE, is more closely related to turnips than to broccoli, and shares the same bitter flavor profile. Its firm texture means it stands up to both quick and long cooking, so go ahead and blanch, sauté, or stew it until it turns army green. No matter how it's cooked, rapini always needs a sidekick to balance its flavor. Here, garlic assumes that role, and I've added some raisins, too, for a little sweetness. If the garlic burns, deep-six it and start over. There is no way to get rid of the horrible flavor and acrid smell, and the extra labor is well worth it.

PREP TIME: **ABOUT 10 MINUTES**
COOKING TIME: **12 TO 18 MINUTES**

Salt

2 pounds rapini (broccoli rabe)

2 tablespoons olive oil

3 garlic cloves, thinly sliced

1 cup golden raisins

1 tablespoon red pepper flakes

1 lemon, sliced

1. Bring a large pot of heavily salted water to a boil. It should be salted enough so that it tastes like the ocean. Set a large metal bowl filled with ice cubes and cold water near the stove. Drop the rapini into the boiling water and blanch for 2 to 3 minutes, or until bright green and tender. It will be slightly undercooked. Lift the rapini from the boiling water and immediately plunge it into the ice bath to stop the cooking. Remove from the ice bath and set aside.

2. In a sauté pan, heat the oil over medium-high heat. Reduce the heat to medium and sauté the garlic just until crispy and golden brown. (Take care that it does not burn.) Add the rapini and sauté for 10 to 15 minutes, or until it is soft and just about melts in your mouth. It will seem overcooked.

3. Season with salt and serve the rapini garnished with the raisins, red pepper flakes, and lemon slices.

Refried Cannellini Beans with Saffron and Garlic {SERVES 6}

I LIKE THE IDEA OF REFRIED BEANS made with just about any bean or legume. For this recipe, I rely on cannellini beans, which are especially creamy, a characteristic that other beans often lack. You have to cook them correctly because God knows there's nothing worse than tough, undercooked beans. I add a little saffron to kick this dish up a few notches, but you can toss in some fresh thyme if you prefer.

PREP TIME: **ABOUT 10 MINUTES**
COOKING TIME: **23 TO 25 MINUTES**

¼ cup olive oil, plus more for drizzling

1 Spanish onion, diced

4 garlic cloves, minced

Pinch of saffron (about 10 threads)

3 cups cooked cannellini beans (see page 203)

3 cups vegetable or chicken stock, preferably homemade

Salt and freshly ground black pepper

Leaves from 4 sprigs fresh oregano

1. In a saucepan or small pot, heat the oil over medium-high heat. When hot, sauté the onion and garlic for 3 to 5 minutes, or until translucent.

2. Take the pan from the heat and add the saffron. Let it infuse the oil mixture for about 5 minutes.

3. Add the beans and return the pan to the heat. Add the broth and bring to a boil. Reduce the heat and simmer for about 20 minutes, or until the broth has reduced by half.

4. Off the heat, mash the beans with a wooden spoon until nearly smooth. This can be rustic and lumpy or very smooth, depending on how you like it. To make it smooth, use a food processor. Season with salt and pepper.

5. Serve drizzled with oil and topped with the oregano.

Grilled Asparagus with Smoked Béarnaise {SERVES 6}

USUALLY YOU FIND ASPARAGUS partying with hollandaise sauce, but after a few drinks, asparagus "experimented" with béarnaise. Happy ending—they discovered they were meant for each other! Remember, béarnaise is nothing more than hollandaise fortified with a white wine–shallot reduction as well as tarragon and chervil. I smoke the butter before adding it to the sauce for extra flavor. It doesn't make sense to smoke less than two pounds of butter at a time because it keeps for a long time and can be used to baste meats, sauté fish, and flavor vegetables with a deep, complex flavor and aroma.

PREP TIME: **10 TO 15 MINUTES**
COOKING TIME: **15 TO 20 MINUTES**

2 tablespoons champagne vinegar

2 tablespoons white wine

1 shallot, sliced

4 sprigs fresh tarragon

1 fresh bay leaf

1½ cups Smoked Butter (recipe follows)

3 large egg yolks

Juice of 1 lemon, or to taste

Salt

1½ teaspoons chopped fresh tarragon, plus more for garnish

1½ teaspoons chopped fresh chervil, plus more for garnish

2 bunches asparagus (12 to 15 spears in each bunch), woody ends removed

Freshly ground black pepper

2 to 3 tablespoons extra-virgin olive oil

1. In a saucepan, combine the vinegar, wine, and ¼ cup of water. Add the shallot, tarragon, and bay leaf and bring to a simmer over medium or medium-high heat. Cook for about 5 minutes, or until reduced by two-thirds.

2. Strain the reduction and then set aside, covered to keep hot.

3. In another pan, melt the smoked butter. If it's already melted, heat it up a little.

4. Transfer the hot shallot reduction to a blender. Add the egg yolks and blend on high speed. Through the feed tube, slowly add the smoked butter, blending until fully emulsified and thick. Season with lemon juice and salt. Remove the blender jar from the base and fold the tarragon and chervil into the béarnaise.

5. Meanwhile, prepare a gas or charcoal grill so that the heating elements or coals are medium-hot.

6. Season the asparagus with salt and pepper and drizzle with olive oil. Grill for 10 to 15 minutes, or until charred and tender, with a little bite.

7. Arrange the asparagus on a platter and spoon the béarnaise over the spears. Pass any extra sauce on the side. Garnish the asparagus with a little more chervil and tarragon.

Smoked Butter {MAKES 2 POUNDS}

PREP TIME: **ABOUT 5 MINUTES, PLUS FREEZING**
COOKING TIME: **15 TO 20 MINUTES OR LONGER DEPENDING ON YOUR SMOKER**

2 pounds (8 sticks) unsalted butter   2 cups applewood chips, for smoking

1. Put the butter in a metal pan in the freezer for 8 to 10 hours or overnight, until the butter is frozen solid and the pan is very cold.

2. Prepare a smoker following the manufacturer's instructions and using the applewood chips. Put the frozen butter, still in the metal pan, in the smoker and smoke for one cycle or until the butter melts.

3. Strain the butter through a fine-mesh sieve or chinois. Use right away or refrigerate for 3 to 4 days until needed. The butter will keep in the freezer for up to three weeks.

BEAN COOKERY 101

Dried beans need to be cooked for a relatively long time before they're edible, and before they're cooked, they need to be soaked in cold water. This makes them something of a pain to prepare (which probably boosts sales of already-cooked canned beans). But bean cookery isn't hard if you plan ahead and give yourself time. Here goes:

Rinse the dried beans, put them in a large pot or bowl, and add enough cold water to cover by two to three inches. Set the beans aside on the kitchen counter (no refrigerator necessary) and go about your business. The beans should soak for at least four hours and can be left all day or overnight.

Drain the soaked beans, which will be visibly swollen, and then put them in a clean pot and again add enough cold water to cover by a few inches. Bring the water to a boil and add a little salt. Not too much, but a little will add good flavor. At this point, foam will rise to the surface of the water; it should be skimmed off and discarded. Reduce the heat to medium-low and simmer the beans very gently until they're done. Check the water level every so often; the beans cook evenly only if covered with several inches of water. To test for doneness, taste a bean. It should be soft enough to squash easily on your tongue but should not be mushy. Drain the beans and proceed with the recipe.

Different beans cook at different rates. For instance, black beans will be done in 40 to 60 minutes, while cannellini beans need 1 to 1½ hours. The age of the beans figures into it as well, with older dried beans (you know that package lurking behind the cans of tomatoes and soup in the back of your pantry, right?) needing more time. So, while it's a production to cook dried beans, it's easy with a little advance work.

Maple Whipped Yams {SERVES 6}

I WANT TO GO ON RECORD saying that maple syrup is perhaps my all-time favorite ingredient. Anything that calls for pure maple syrup makes me think of New England, where the winters are cold and snowy and slowly melt into a chilly spring—time to button up your flannel shirt and grab the sap buckets.

The maple syrup goes well with lots of things, but nothing tops its relationship with the lowly yam. Both are naturally sweet, and when paired they bring out the best in each other. This recipe is super simple and super yummy. If you want to switch out the yam, you can use paler-hued sweet potatoes, parsnips, or even carrots.

PREP TIME: **ABOUT 10 MINUTES**
COOKING TIME: **ABOUT 55 MINUTES**

2 pounds yams

4 cups heavy cream

2 cups maple syrup

1 teaspoon ground cinnamon

½ teaspoon ground allspice

½ teaspoon freshly grated nutmeg

½ teaspoon ground cloves

2 cups whole milk or heavy cream, at room temperature (or mix the cream and milk to make this as rich as you like)

4 tablespoons (½ stick) unsalted butter, sliced

Leaves from 1 sprig fresh rosemary, chopped

1. Preheat the oven to 350°F.

2. Wrap the yams individually in aluminum foil and bake for about 30 minutes, or until tender when pierced with a fork. Remove from the oven but do not turn the oven off.

3. Meanwhile, in a saucepan, heat the cream, maple syrup, cinnamon, allspice, nutmeg, and cloves over medium-high heat until rapidly simmering. Reduce the heat and simmer for about 15 minutes, or until reduced by half. Adjust the heat up or down to maintain the simmer.

4. Split the yams open and spoon the flesh into the saucepan with the flavored cream. Simmer, stirring, for about 10 minutes, or until smooth enough to mash.

5. Transfer to the bowl of a food processor fitted with the metal blade, add the milk, and process until silky smooth.

6. Spoon the yams into six individual ramekins or a casserole dish and top with slices of butter. Return the yams to the oven and let them heat until very hot and the butter melts. Serve garnished with the rosemary.

7
SWEET TREATS

GIVE ME CHOCOLATE, give me vanilla, give me caramel . . . these are the words that'll most likely end up on my gravestone. I swear to God, there are few things in life that I'm more a slave to than all things sweet.

These recipes are trickier for me than the others in the book, simply because I am much more comfortable with the savory side of cooking. Because of this, they're easy to reproduce in your home kitchen. If I can master 'em, so can you. Like the recipes in the Grains and Pasta and Other Good Things chapter, there is less gray area when it comes to prep. These guys demand your attention, technique-wise. As far as flavor combos, the world is your oyster (or should I say sugar bowl?). Feel free to play around with spices, nuts, or whatever in an attempt to make these your own.

It's important to remember that there are a lot of things you can't fool with, like the oven temperature, how long something rests or bakes, how you incorporate ingredients, and all that noise. So, play it safe the first time you make the recipes, then when you're more confident, go back and mess around to your heart's content.

Carrot Cake with Cream Cheese Frosting {SERVES 8 TO 10}

ONE OF MY ALL-TIME favorite desserts, carrot cake illustrates how an ingredient mostly thought of for savory preparations does an about-face and shines in a sweet one. If you wanna get creative, switch out the carrots with parsnips and show everyone how imaginative you are. You can also flavor the cream cheese frosting with spices, nuts, or even herbs if you're feeling crazy.

PREP TIME: 30 TO 35 MINUTES
COOKING TIME: ABOUT 30 MINUTES

CAKE

12 ounces (3 sticks) unsalted butter, at room temperature, plus more for the pans

2½ cups all-purpose flour, plus more for the pans

2 teaspoons salt

1 teaspoon baking powder

1 teaspoon baking soda

1 teaspoon ground cinnamon

½ teaspoon ground ginger

½ teaspoon freshly grated nutmeg

1 cup firmly packed dark brown sugar

½ cup granulated sugar

3 large eggs

8 to 10 medium carrots, peeled and shredded on a box grater

½ cup fresh orange juice (from 2 to 3 oranges)

2 teaspoons pure vanilla extract

1½ cups currants

CREAM CHEESE FROSTING

2 (8-ounce) packages cream cheese, at room temperature

2 teaspoons pure vanilla extract

8 ounces (2 sticks) unsalted butter, at room temperature, cut into pieces

2 pounds confectioners' sugar, sifted

1. For the cake, preheat the oven to 350°F. Butter two 9-inch round cake pans and dust with flour. Tap out the excess flour.

2. In a large bowl, whisk the flour, salt, baking powder, baking soda, cinnamon, ginger, and nutmeg.

3. In the bowl of a stand mixer fitted with the paddle attachment, beat the butter, brown sugar, and granulated sugar on medium speed for 5 to 6 minutes, or until lightened and fluffy. Add the eggs one at a time, beating well after each addition.

4. Add the grated carrots, orange juice, and vanilla and beat to mix well. With the mixer on low speed, add the flour mixture, a little at a time. When the flour is incorporated, stir in the currants.

5. Scrape the batter into the prepared pans, dividing it evenly. Bake for about 30 minutes, or until toothpicks inserted into the centers of the cakes come out clean. Rotate the position of the pans halfway through baking.

6. Let the cakes cool in the pans set on wire racks for about 15 minutes. Run a dull knife between the cakes and the sides of the pans and then invert the cakes onto wire racks. Turn right side up and let the cakes cool completely.

7. For the cream cheese frosting, in the bowl of a stand mixer fitted with the paddle attachment, beat the cream cheese and vanilla on medium-high speed for about 2 minutes, or until light and creamy. Reduce the speed to medium and gradually add the butter, beating until smooth.

8. Reduce the speed to low and very gradually add the confectioners' sugar. Beat until fully incorporated.

9. Trim the rounded tops of the cake layers with a serrated knife so that they are flat. Spread about 1 cup of the frosting on a trimmed cake layer. Top with the second layer and spread the remaining frosting over the top and sides. Refrigerate the frosted cake for at least 1 hour before serving.

Green Apple Rosemary Sorbet
{SERVES 4 TO 6; MAKES ABOUT 1 QUART}

SORBET IS EASY TO MAKE, and honestly, it doesn't get more effortless than this. Apples and rosemary—two pals that go together with such bravado, it's a wonder they haven't been asked to make a buddy-cop movie! They're a perfect balance of tart and sweet, with the floral notes inherent to rosemary backing up the apple, making them perfect for sorbet. For more concentrated flavors, reduce a cup or so of apple cider with some rosemary in the pan until it turns into a rich, heady syrup that can be added to the sorbet before it's frozen, or serve it as a topping at the table.

PREP TIME: **ABOUT 10 MINUTES, PLUS FREEZING**
COOKING TIME: **8 TO 10 MINUTES**

⅔ cup sugar

3 sprigs fresh rosemary

6 Granny Smith apples, or other firm, tart apples

Juice of 1 lemon

2 teaspoons salt

1. In a saucepan, combine the sugar with ⅓ cup of water. Add the rosemary sprigs and bring to a boil, stirring until the sugar has dissolved and the syrup is clear. Remove from the heat and let the syrup cool to room temperature. Strain out the rosemary.

2. Peel, core, and coarsely chop the apples and transfer to a blender. Add the cooled simple syrup and lemon juice. Blend until smooth and then season with the salt.

3. Transfer the mixture to an ice cream machine and freeze according to the manufacturer's instructions. When frozen, the sorbet will be soft but ready to eat. For firmer sorbet, or to store it until needed, spoon it into a freezer-safe container (metal is best) and freeze for at least 2 hours and up to several days.

Bananas Foster Crème Brûlée {SERVES 6}

THIS IS AN EPIC culinary mash-up, one that should be cooked in the gastronomic octagon, MMA style! In one corner you have the Caribbean-inspired bananas Foster. In the other, the yummy yet predictable old standby, crème brûlée. Let 'em duke it out and what are you left with? Bananas Foster Crème Brûlée, aka ridiculous deliciousness. The resulting dish is actually better than either of the contenders alone. This is a delightful example of how it can be okay to mess around with "fusion"—as long as it doesn't turn into confusion.

PREP TIME: ABOUT 10 MINUTES, PLUS CHILLING
COOKING TIME: 50 TO 60 MINUTES

1 tablespoon unsalted butter	3 cups heavy cream
3 bananas, chopped	1 vanilla bean, split lengthwise, or 1 teaspoon pure vanilla extract
4 tablespoons light brown sugar	8 large egg yolks
2 teaspoons fresh lemon juice	5 tablespoons granulated sugar
¼ cup dark rum	

1. Preheat the oven to 300ºF.

2. In a sauté pan, melt the butter over medium heat. When melted, add the bananas. Sprinkle with 1 tablespoon of the brown sugar and stir well to blend the sugar with the butter and bananas. Cook, stirring occasionally, for 5 minutes, or until the bananas are slightly caramelized. Mash them with a wooden spoon until as smooth as possible.

3. Add the lemon juice, raise the heat to medium-high, and add the rum. Let the mixture come to a boil and cook for 1 minute. Remove from the heat and divide the bananas among six ramekins or custard cups.

4. Pour the cream into a saucepan and scrape the seeds from the vanilla bean into the cream. Bring to a boil over medium-high heat. As soon as it boils, remove from the heat.

5. In the top of a double boiler set over simmering water, whisk the egg yolks with the granulated sugar until the mixture thickens. Strain the cream into the egg yolks and continue to stir for about 10 minutes, until the custard thickens enough to coat the back of a wooden spoon. Ladle the hot custard over the bananas in the ramekins, dividing it evenly, and transfer the ramekins to a roasting pan large enough to hold them without touching.

6. Put the roasting pan on the center rack of the oven and pour in hot water to come halfway up the sides of the ramekins. Bake for about 40 minutes, or until the custards are set.

7. Lift the custards from the roasting pan and let them cool. Refrigerate for 3 hours to 12 hours.

8. Just before serving, sprinkle the remaining brown sugar evenly over the custards and caramelize with a small blowtorch or under the broiler. Serve while the sugar crust is still hot.

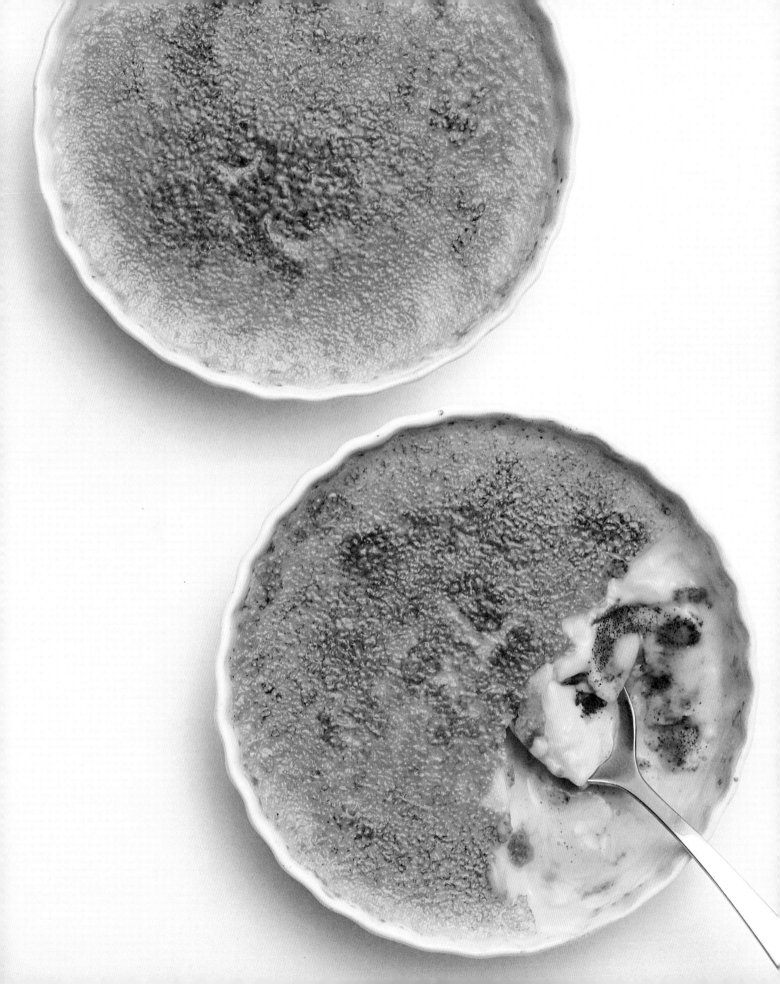

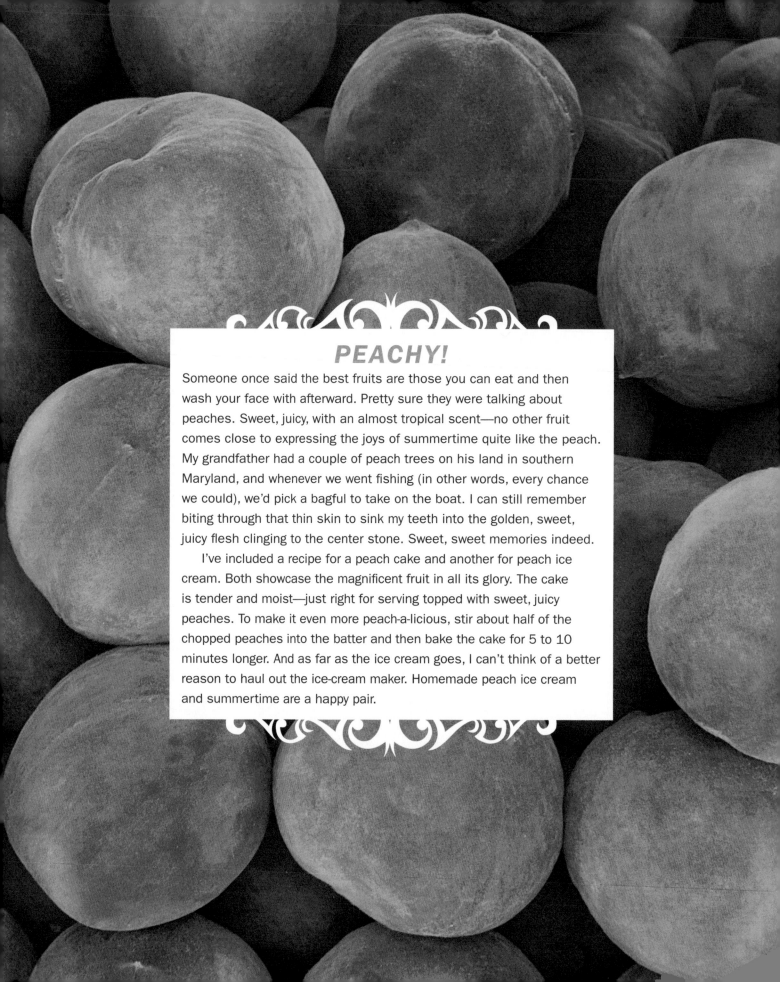

PEACHY!

Someone once said the best fruits are those you can eat and then wash your face with afterward. Pretty sure they were talking about peaches. Sweet, juicy, with an almost tropical scent—no other fruit comes close to expressing the joys of summertime quite like the peach. My grandfather had a couple of peach trees on his land in southern Maryland, and whenever we went fishing (in other words, every chance we could), we'd pick a bagful to take on the boat. I can still remember biting through that thin skin to sink my teeth into the golden, sweet, juicy flesh clinging to the center stone. Sweet, sweet memories indeed.

I've included a recipe for a peach cake and another for peach ice cream. Both showcase the magnificent fruit in all its glory. The cake is tender and moist—just right for serving topped with sweet, juicy peaches. To make it even more peach-a-licious, stir about half of the chopped peaches into the batter and then bake the cake for 5 to 10 minutes longer. And as far as the ice cream goes, I can't think of a better reason to haul out the ice-cream maker. Homemade peach ice cream and summertime are a happy pair.

Peach Ice Cream {SERVES 8}

PREP TIME: **ABOUT 20 MINUTES, PLUS MACERATING AND FREEZING**
COOKING TIME: **ABOUT 15 MINUTES**

1½ pounds peaches (3 large), peeled and coarsely chopped

1 tablespoon brandy

½ cup heavy cream

¼ cup whole milk

¼ cup half-and-half

1 vanilla bean, split lengthwise, or ½ teaspoon pure vanilla extract

2 large egg yolks

¼ cup packed dark brown sugar

½ cup crème fraîche

1. Put the peaches in a large bowl and sprinkle with the brandy. Stir gently and set aside to macerate for at least 1 hour but no longer than 4 hours.

2. Transfer the peaches to the bowl of a food processor fitted with the metal blade or a blender and pulse until smooth.

3. In a large saucepan, mix the cream, milk, and half-and-half. Scrape the vanilla seeds into the pan and then drop in the vanilla pod. Bring to a simmer over medium heat. Remove from the heat and pour through a fine-mesh sieve into a bowl to strain out the vanilla pod and seeds.

4. In a large saucepan, whisk the egg yolks and brown sugar. Add the milk mixture, whisking continuously to blend. Set the saucepan over medium heat and cook for about 15 minutes, stirring continuously, until the custard thickens and coats the back of a wooden spoon. Meanwhile, fill a large metal bowl with ice cubes and cold water and set it near the stove.

5. Remove the custard from the heat and strain again through a fine-mesh sieve into a metal bowl. Set the bowl in the ice bath to cool. When cold, stir in the pureed peaches and crème fraîche. Cover and refrigerate for at least 6 hours and up to 12 hours.

6. When very cold, transfer the custard to an ice-cream machine and process according to the manufacturer's instructions. Transfer the churned ice cream to a freezer-safe container and freeze for at least 3 hours before serving.

Summer Peach Cake {SERVES 12}

PREP TIME: **ABOUT 10 MINUTES**
COOKING TIME: **30 TO 35 MINUTES**

8 tablespoons (1 stick) unsalted butter, plus more for the pan

4 large, juicy peaches, peeled and sliced into wedges

¼ cup plus 2 tablespoons granulated sugar

2 teaspoons ground cinnamon

2 cups all-purpose flour

1 teaspoon salt

1 teaspoon baking soda

1½ cups packed light brown sugar

1 large egg

1 cup buttermilk

1. Preheat the oven to 350°F. Butter a 9 x 13-inch baking pan.

2. In a small bowl, whisk the granulated sugar and cinnamon. Set aside all but 2 generous tablespoons.

3. Put the peaches in a glass or ceramic bowl and sprinkle them with the 2 tablespoons of cinnamon sugar. Toss gently, cover the bowl, and refrigerate until 30 minutes before serving.

4. In a medium bowl, sift the flour, salt, and baking soda.

5. In the bowl of a stand mixer fitted with the paddle attachment, cream the brown sugar and butter on medium-high speed for 3 to 4 minutes, or until light and fluffy. Add the egg and beat until incorporated.

6. With the mixer on low speed, slowly add the flour mixture, alternating with the buttermilk. Mix until the batter is smooth.

7. Remove the bowl from the mixer and spread the batter in the pan, smoothing it as evenly as possible.

8. Sprinkle the reserved cinnamon sugar over the batter. Bake for 30 to 35 minutes, or until a toothpick inserted into the center of the cake comes out clean. Set the pan on a wire rack to cool completely before cutting into squares. Serve the cake squares with the peaches spooned over them.

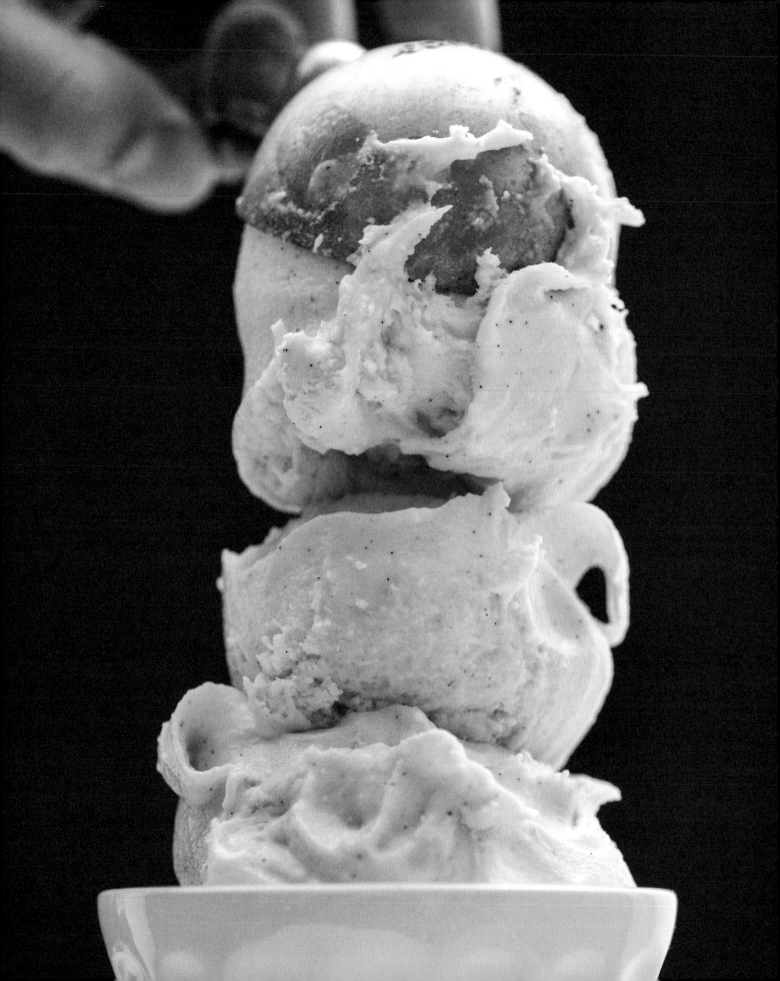

Not-Your-Grandma's Vanilla Ice Cream

{SERVES 8}

HOW MANY TIMES have you heard something that's BOR-ing being described as "vanilla"? In fact, there's absolutely nothing boring about vanilla. Intoxicatingly fragrant vanilla beans come from stunningly beautiful orchids that grow in the tropical forests of Madagascar and Tahiti. What could be more exotic? Lick this ice cream off your spoon and you'll never again think of vanilla as being ordinary or dull!

PREP TIME: **ABOUT 20 MINUTES, PLUS INFUSING AND FREEZING**
COOKING TIME: **ABOUT 10 MINUTES**

2 cups heavy cream

2 cups half-and-half

2 vanilla beans, split lengthwise, or 1 teaspoon pure vanilla extract

9 large egg yolks

1 cup sugar

1 tablespoon salt

1. In a large saucepan, mix the cream and half-and-half. Scrape the vanilla seeds into the pan and then drop the vanilla pods into the pan. Bring to a gentle boil over medium heat and immediately remove from the heat. Set aside for 30 minutes to give the vanilla time to infuse the cream.

2. In a medium bowl, whisk the egg yolks until they lighten in color. Gradually add the sugar and salt, whisking continuously to combine.

3. Return the saucepan with the cream to medium heat and bring to a simmer. Meanwhile, fill a metal bowl with ice cubes and cold water and set it near the stove.

4. Pour about one-third of the hot cream into the yolks, whisking continuously to keep the eggs from scrambling and the custard smooth. Pour the cream and yolks into the saucepan with the remaining cream and set over low heat. Cook for 3 to 5 minutes, until the custard thickens slightly and coats the back of a wooden spoon. When you draw a finger across the custard on the spoon, it should leave a line.

5. Strain the custard through a fine-mesh sieve into a metal bowl to remove the vanilla beans and seeds. Put the bowl in the ice bath and let the custard cool until chilled.

6. Transfer the custard to an ice-cream maker and churn following the manufacturer's instructions. Serve at once or transfer the churned ice cream to freezer-safe containers and freeze for at least 3 hours, or until hard.

Lemon-Blueberry Bars

{SERVES 8 TO 10; MAKES 20 BARS}

AH, YES: LEMON AND BLUEBERRIES. What a perfect embodiment of fruity happiness this pair is. The simple, crusty bars scream "summer" to me, and because there are so few ingredients, make sure to use fruit at the peak of perfection: bright yellow, juicy lemons, and blueberries that burst at the seams, like Violet Beauregarde in *Willy Wonka & the Chocolate Factory*. Feel free to switch ingredients around. Instead of lemons, use clementines, pomelos, or tangerines. Instead of blueberries, try blackberries or gooseberries . . . or snozberries, if you can find 'em!

PREP TIME: **15 TO 18 MINUTES, PLUS CHILLING**
COOKING TIME: **45 TO 50 MINUTES**

CRUST

- 8 ounces (2 sticks) unsalted butter, at room temperature
- ½ cup granulated sugar
- 2 cups all-purpose flour, plus more for dusting
- 2 teaspoons salt

FILLING

- 6 large eggs
- 3 cups granulated sugar
- 1 cup all-purpose flour
- 2 tablespoons grated lemon zest (from 4 to 6 lemons)
- 1 cup fresh lemon juice (from 3 to 4 lemons)
- 1 pint fresh blueberries
- About 1 cup confectioners' sugar, for dusting (optional)

1. For the crust, in the bowl of a stand mixer fitted with the paddle attachment, beat the butter and granulated sugar on medium speed for 5 to 6 minutes, or until light and fluffy. With the mixer on low speed, add the flour and salt and mix just until combined.

2. Turn the dough out onto a lightly floured surface and gather it together into a ball. Press the dough into a 9 x 13-inch rimmed baking pan, pushing the dough ½ inch up the sides. Refrigerate for 30 minutes.

3. Preheat the oven to 350°F.

4. Bake the crust for 15 to 20 minutes, or until very lightly browned. Set the pan on a wire rack to cool. Do not turn off the oven.

5. For the filling, in a large bowl, whisk the eggs, granulated sugar, flour, lemon zest, and lemon juice until smooth. Gently stir the blueberries into the batter, taking care not to break or crush them. Pour the batter into the cooled crust and bake for about 30 minutes, or until the filling is set.

6. Let the bars cool in the pan set on a wire rack until room temperature. Cut into bars and dust with confectioners' sugar, if desired.

S'Mores Pie {SERVES 8}

GRAHAM CRACKERS (no, I wasn't named after them; for the record, I was named for Graham Nash), marshmallows, and chocolate—three uncomplicated ingredients that form a foodie ménage à trois, if you will. Not much more needs to be said about this one beyond that it's downright tasty and will resonate with anyone who has ever spent a summer evening outdoors around a campfire with a gooey marshmallow clinging to the end of a stick. Yummy childhood innocence.

PREP TIME: 15 TO 20 MINUTES, PLUS CHILLING
COOKING TIME: 14 TO 15 MINUTES

GRAHAM CRACKER CRUST

- 1½ cups graham cracker crumbs (from 12 to 13 whole graham crackers)
- ¼ cup packed light brown sugar
- 1 teaspoon salt
- ½ teaspoon ground cinnamon
- 7 tablespoons unsalted butter, melted

FILLING

- 1 cup sugar
- ½ cup all-purpose flour
- 2 teaspoons salt
- 3 cups whole milk
- 3 ounces bittersweet or semisweet chocolate, coarsely chopped
- 4 large egg yolks
- 1 tablespoon unsalted butter
- 1½ teaspoons pure vanilla extract

MERINGUE

- 1¼ cups plus 2½ tablespoons sugar
- 3 large egg whites, at room temperature

1. For the graham cracker crust, in a large bowl, toss the graham cracker crumbs with the brown sugar, salt, and cinnamon. Add the butter and stir with a fork until the crumbs are moist and sticking together.

2. Press the crust mixture into the bottom and up the sides of a 9-inch pie plate. Press hard to ensure a compact crust. Chill the crust for at least 1 hour or up to 12 hours.

3. For the filling, in a saucepan, whisk the sugar, flour, and salt. Whisk in the milk and then add the chocolate. Set the pan over medium-high heat and cook, stirring continuously, for 4 to 5 minutes, or until the chocolate has melted and the mixture is thickened and bubbling. Without stirring, cook for 2 minutes longer. Remove the pan from the heat.

4. In a medium bowl, whisk the egg yolks. Slowly pour the hot milk mixture into them, whisking continuously to prevent them from scrambling. Return the mixture to the saucepan and bring to a gentle boil. Cook, stirring, for about 2 minutes longer, or until the pastry cream is smooth and thick.

5. Remove the saucepan from the heat and stir in the butter and vanilla. When the pastry cream is completely smooth and still warm, pour it into the chilled graham cracker crust. Cover the filled pie with plastic wrap and chill for at least 3 hours.

6. Just before serving, make the meringue. In a medium saucepan, whisk 1¼ cups of the sugar with 5 tablespoons of water. Cook, stirring, until the sugar has dissolved. Stop stirring and let the syrup heat until it registers 220ºF on a candy thermometer. Set the syrup aside.

7. Meanwhile, in the bowl of a stand mixer fitted with the whisk attachment, whip the egg whites on medium speed until foamy. With the mixer running, gradually add the remaining 2½ tablespoons sugar. Increase the speed to medium-high and whip the whites until they form soft peaks (the meringue folds back on itself when the beater is lifted).

8. With the mixer still running, slowly add the sugar syrup. Pour it down the side of the bowl to avoid the whisk and scrape the bowl down with a rubber spatula a few times, if necessary. Continue to beat until stiff peaks form and the bowl is cool to the touch.

9. Pile the meringue over the chilled chocolate pie filling. Make sure it touches the crust all around the pie plate and swirl it in an attractive pattern. Using a small blowtorch, brown the tips of the swirled meringue, adjusting the flame to ensure even browning, or slide the pie under the broiler just long enough to lightly brown the tips of the meringue. Serve right away.

Nontraditional Banana Split {SERVES 1}

FOOD HAS THE UNCANNY ABILITY to connect us to the past. When I think of banana splits, I am immediately transported to a more innocent America, circa 1950, when soda jerks reigned in ice cream parlors. I was born in 1977, so clearly I have no firsthand experience of the 1950s, but this goes to show the magical power of culinary history.

I've lifted this old-time favorite out of its time and brûléed the bananas to give them an ever-so-slight crunchiness along with rich caramelization. I've substituted sweet, chewy hazelnut clusters for the peanuts to coax out deeper flavor, and then created a rich and sensual chocolate sauce that's spiked with coffee. The whipped cream is beaten just before serving—never from a can with a squirt nozzle—and flavored with a smidge of sugar so that it tastes like (guess what?) cream!

PREP TIME: **ABOUT 8 MINUTES**
COOKING TIME: **2 TO 3 MINUTES**

- 1 large banana
- 1 to 2 tablespoons raw sugar
- 2 scoops Not-Your-Grandma's Vanilla Ice Cream (page 219)
- 3 to 4 tablespoons Coffee-Chocolate Sauce (recipe follows)
- 1 or 2 Caramelized Hazelnut Clusters (recipe follows)
- 1 or 2 store-bought pretzels, crushed
- 2 to 3 dollops Sweetened Whipped Cream (recipe follows)
- 1 maraschino cherry

1. Preheat the broiler.

2. Split the banana in half lengthwise. Put the halves on a baking sheet lined with aluminum foil and sprinkle with the raw sugar. Broil for 1 to 3 minutes, until the sugar caramelizes.

3. Put the banana halves on either side of a large serving dish (an oval one works well). Put the scoops of ice cream in the center of the dish. Top with the chocolate sauce, hazelnut clusters, and crushed pretzels. Spoon the whipped cream on top of the ice cream and top with the cherry. Serve at once.

Coffee-Chocolate Sauce {MAKES ABOUT 4 CUPS}

PREP TIME: **ABOUT 8 MINUTES**
COOKING TIME: **6 TO 7 MINUTES**

2 cups sugar

1¼ cups corn syrup

1½ cups brewed coffee, at room temperature

½ cup natural (nonalkalized) unsweetened cocoa powder

2 teaspoons salt

1. In a large saucepan, stir the sugar, corn syrup, and 1 cup cold water and heat over medium-high heat, stirring to prevent the sugar from burning. Bring to a boil and let the mixture cook without stirring until the syrup turns amber. Remove from the heat.

2. In a small bowl, whisk the coffee and cocoa powder. Add the coffee mixture to the syrup (the mixture will bubble, so take care) and heat over low heat, stirring until smooth. Add the salt and stir to combine. (If the syrup hardens before you have a chance to mix it with the coffee, let it soften over low heat until liquid.)

3. Serve the sauce immediately or transfer to a lidded container and refrigerate for up to 5 days. Reheat before using.

Caramelized Hazelnut Clusters {MAKES 4 CUPS}

PREP TIME: **3 TO 4 MINUTES**
COOKING TIME: **13 TO 15 MINUTES**

Cooking spray or butter, for the pan

3 cups whole or halved hazelnuts

½ cup sugar

2 tablespoons unsalted butter

2 teaspoons salt

1. Preheat the oven to 325°F. Line a baking sheet with aluminum foil and spray it with cooking spray or butter it.

2. Spread the nuts evenly in a shallow baking pan and roast for about 10 minutes, stirring once.

3. In a medium saucepan, heat the sugar over medium-high heat and let the sugar melt without stirring. Shake the pan several times to encourage even melting. When the sugar melts and looks syrupy, add the butter and stir until smooth and entirely melted. Remove the pan from the heat.

4. Add the roasted nuts to the pan, stirring to coat evenly. Pour the nut mixture on the prepared baking sheet and then sprinkle with the salt. Set aside to cool completely.

5. When cool, break the nuts into clusters and store in a lidded container at room temperature for up to 3 weeks. You can freeze the nut clusters for up to 3 months.

Sweetened Whipped Cream {MAKES ABOUT 1½ CUPS}

PREP TIME: 5 TO 7 MINUTES

1 cup heavy cream

2 tablespoons confectioners' sugar

½ teaspoon pure vanilla extract

1. In the bowl of a stand mixer fitted with the whisk attachment, beat the cream and sugar on high speed until stiff peaks form. Add the vanilla and beat just to combine.

2. Use immediately or refrigerate in an airtight container until needed. Rewhip for 1 minute before using.

Bourbon Brownies {SERVES 12}

I'M ALWAYS INTERESTED in the history of classics, and both bourbon and brownies boast that moniker. Bourbon is one of America's greatest products, made with love and care and appreciated by those with sophisticated palates. It showcases the resourcefulness of the Kentucky-Tennessee Appalachian region and embodies our country in every sense of the word. My old man is a bourbon drinker, one of those guys who likes to swirl it around in the glass, inspecting the color and appreciating the aroma before he sips, much like wine aficionados do with their red juice. Brownies are another all-American great that have been exported to the far reaches of the world, filling kitchens from Kalamazoo to Timbuktu with delectable scents. Put them together with bourbon, and you're in heaven.

PREP TIME: 10 TO 15 MINUTES
COOKING TIME: ABOUT 35 MINUTES

Cooking spray

1 pound bittersweet chocolate, coarsely chopped

8 ounces (2 sticks) unsalted butter

½ cup bourbon

2½ cups granulated sugar

2 large eggs

2 teaspoons pure vanilla extract

1 cup all-purpose flour

1 teaspoon salt

Confectioners' sugar, for dusting (optional)

1. Preheat the oven to 350°F. Spray a 9 x 13-inch baking pan with cooking spray.

2. In the top of a double boiler, melt the chocolate and butter over simmering water, stirring until smooth and completely mixed. Stir in the bourbon. Transfer the chocolate mixture to the bowl of a stand mixer fitted with the paddle attachment. Add the sugar and beat on medium-high speed until smooth. Add the eggs one at a time, making sure each is incorporated before adding the next. Add the vanilla and beat until mixed.

3. In a mixing bowl, whisk the flour and salt. Add to the batter and beat just until combined. Scrape the batter into the prepared pan and bake for about 30 minutes, or until a toothpick inserted into the center comes out clean.

4. Set the pan on a wire rack to cool. Sprinkle the brownies with confectioners' sugar, if desired. Cut into squares and serve.

Panna Cotta with Stewed Raspberries

{SERVES 8}

PANNA COTTA TRANSLATES to "cooked cream," but the custard is not really cooked, just warmed. If you don't have much of a sense of what it is, think of crème brûlée without the eggs and without the crunchy, burnt-sugar crust. In other words, not like crème brûlée at all, except that it and panna cotta share a tempting custardy texture. For panna cotta, this is achieved with gelatin, added when the cream is warm so that it dissolves easily, and then allowed to set as it cools.

I serve panna cotta with fresh berries; their mild acidity cuts through the richness of the cream. Citrus also works well with panna cotta, so it's up to you in which direction you wanna head.

PREP TIME: ABOUT 25 MINUTES, PLUS STEEPING AND CHILLING
COOKING TIME: 5 TO 8 MINUTES

PANNA COTTA

- 4 cups heavy cream
- ½ cup sugar
- 1 teaspoon salt
- 1 vanilla bean, split lengthwise, or 1 teaspoon pure vanilla extract
- 2¼ teaspoons powdered gelatin

STEWED RASPBERRIES

- 2 pints raspberries
- ½ cup sugar
- 2 tablespoons sweet wine (such as Sauternes, white Riesling, Chenin Blanc, or Moscatel)
- Fresh mint, for garnish

1. For the panna cotta, in a medium saucepan, whisk the cream, sugar, and salt. Scrape the seeds from the vanilla bean into the cream and drop the vanilla bean into the pan. Bring to a simmer over medium heat and then immediately remove from the heat. Cover the saucepan with plastic wrap or a tight-fitting lid and set aside to steep for about 10 minutes.

2. Put 3 tablespoons of water in a small bowl and sprinkle the gelatin over it. Let stand for about 5 minutes to soften the gelatin.

3. Strain the cream through a fine-mesh sieve into a saucepan to remove the vanilla pod and seeds.

4. Bring the cream to a simmer over medium heat and then immediately remove from the heat. Stir the gelatin into the cream, whisking until fully dissolved.

5. Pour the cream into eight 4-ounce ramekins or custard cups. Let cool to room temperature. Cover the ramekins with plastic wrap and refrigerate for about 4 hours until firm.

6. For the stewed raspberries, in a bowl, toss the raspberries with the sugar and wine. Cover and refrigerate for about 1 hour so that the juices are drawn from the berries.

7. Serve the panna cotta in the ramekins with small spoonfuls of the raspberries on top. Garnish with mint, if desired, and serve.

Lemon Ricotta Fritters {MAKES 36 FRITTERS}

NO REASON TO BE snooty when it comes to fried food. Crunchy, crispy, simple, and yummy. Just as food should be. Serve these fritters with nothing more than confectioners' sugar as suggested here, or how about lemon curd or blackberry jam? Yummy!

I make these with a goodly amount of ricotta cheese. "Ricotta" means "re-cooked," because the easygoing creamy cheese is made from the whey once it's removed from the curd (a process that also makes ricotta less fatty than other cheeses). Its sweet creaminess means it pairs well with both sweet and savory preparations. Here, it's paired with lemons, which, like ricotta, seem to go well with pretty much every other food under the sun. No surprise that together they harmonize like a church choir on Sunday morning. Go forth and fry!

PREP TIME: **ABOUT 10 MINUTES**
COOKING TIME: **6 TO 9 MINUTES DEPENDING ON THE NUMBER OF BATCHES**

About 4 cups vegetable oil, for frying

1 cup all-purpose flour

2 tablespoons grated lemon zest

1 tablespoon baking powder

1 teaspoon salt

1 pound sheep's-milk ricotta cheese, drained (about 2 cups)

4 large eggs

¼ cup granulated sugar

1½ teaspoons pure vanilla extract

Confectioners' sugar, for dusting

1. In a large, wide, heavy saucepan, pour enough oil to reach a depth of about 1½ inches. Heat the oil over high heat until it registers 370°F on a deep-fry thermometer.

2. Meanwhile, in a medium bowl, whisk the flour, lemon zest, baking powder, and salt.

3. In a separate large bowl, whisk the ricotta, eggs, granulated sugar, and vanilla. When smooth and well blended, fold in the flour mixture and whisk to mix well.

4. Working in batches, gently drop a level tablespoon of the batter into the hot oil. Fry for about 3 minutes, turning the fritters a few times, until deeply golden brown. Lift the fritters from the oil and drain them on paper towels. Let the oil come back to temperature between batches.

5. Dust generously with confectioners' sugar and serve warm.

Spiced Krispies Treats {SERVES 6}

WHO HASN'T HAD A LOVE AFFAIR with traditional Rice Krispies Treats? Warm, gooey, buttery, sweet . . . what could be better? Answer: these guys! I get a kick out of taking everyday dishes and putting a twist on 'em. In this case, I added some autumn baking spices to the mix to come up with an amazing version of the classic treat. The real trick is the brown butter. By toasting it a little longer than usual, its natural sugars caramelize and fill the kitchen with the most intoxicating aroma any kitchen can have.

PREP TIME: 10 TO 15 MINUTES
COOKING TIME: 8 TO 10 MINUTES

6 tablespoons (¾ stick) unsalted butter, plus more for the pan

Cooking spray, for the pan (optional)

2 teaspoons ground cinnamon

½ teaspoon freshly grated nutmeg

½ teaspoon ground allspice

½ teaspoon ground cardamom

¼ teaspoon ground ginger

¼ teaspoon kosher salt

1 (10-ounce) bag marshmallows (38 to 40 marshmallows)

6 cups Rice Krispies or other crisped rice cereal

1 teaspoon fleur de sel or other pure, large-grain salt (see page 88)

1. Lightly butter a 9 x 13-inch shallow baking pan, or spray it with cooking spray. Set aside.

2. In a saucepan, melt the butter over medium-high heat. Cook for 2 to 3 minutes after it has melted, or until it browns and has a nutty aroma.

3. Remove the pan from the heat and add the cinnamon, nutmeg, allspice, cardamom, ginger, and kosher salt. Stir to coat the spices with butter, return to low heat, and toast slightly for 3 to 5 minutes.

4. Add the marshmallows and cook gently to allow the marshmallows to melt.

5. Put the Rice Krispies in a large bowl and scrape the melted marshmallow mixture into the bowl. Using a wooden spoon or a lightly buttered rubber spatula, mix until the cereal is coated with marshmallows.

6. Spread the mixture into the prepared pan and press it evenly into the pan. Sprinkle with the fleur de sel and let the treats sit for about 15 minutes. Cut into the desired size squares or rectangles.

Sugar Cookies {MAKES 20 COOKIES}

AT THE END OF THE DAY, recipes essentially are blueprints that a cook or baker uses as a foundation. The sugar cookie personifies this concept as the basis for nearly every cookie you'll ever make, particularly those you decorate at Halloween, Christmas, or Valentine's Day.

While I usually like to mess around with the classics to make them stand out, at times the purist in me fights back. This is what happens with sugar cookies. Rather than add spices, flavorings, or colorings to the dough, I bake the cookies as written here, and always with good results. If I'm in the mood to go a little crazy, I might tweak the frosting or decorations. But as the Wu-Tang Clan says, "Sugar cookies ain't nuthin' to f**k with!" Agreed.

PREP TIME: **ABOUT 12 MINUTES**
COOKING TIME: **ABOUT 15 MINUTES**

2 cups granulated sugar

¼ cup packed light brown sugar

8 ounces (2 sticks) unsalted butter, slightly softened

2 large eggs

2 teaspoons pure vanilla extract

3 cups all-purpose flour

1 teaspoon salt

1 teaspoon baking soda

1. Preheat the oven to 350°F. Line two baking sheets with parchment paper. (If you don't have parchment paper, butter the baking sheets.)

2. In the bowl of a stand mixer fitted with the paddle attachment, beat 1¾ cups of the granulated sugar, the brown sugar, and the butter on medium-high speed for about 2 minutes, or until light and fluffy. Scrape down the sides of the bowl as needed during mixing.

3. Add the eggs and vanilla and beat until blended.

4. In a medium bowl, whisk the flour, salt, and baking soda. With the mixer on low speed, slowly add the flour mixture just until it's incorporated into the batter.

5. Spread the remaining ¼ cup granulated sugar in a shallow dish. Using a 2-inch ice cream scoop, scoop up balls of batter and roll them in the sugar. Put them about 2 inches apart on the lined baking sheets and flatten them slightly. Bake for about 15 minutes, or until lightly browned around the edges.

6. Let the cookies rest on the baking sheets for 2 or 3 minutes and then transfer to wire racks to cool. Serve right away or store in an airtight container for up to 3 days.

Acknowledgments

When I've read the acknowledgment pages in other books, I've wondered who all those people were. Why so many to get one book written? Now I know! Writing a cookbook such as this is far from a solo activity. So from the bottom of my heart I want to thank the following folks. Without them this book might not have been a reality:

To Merlin Verrier, the Abbot to my Costello, the Frank to my Sinatra, the French to my Laundry . . . you've been my BFF since day one and words can't sum up what you mean to me. To those who busted their assets to help make this cookbook possible—and I'm talking about you, David Fingerman, Jacob Saben, and Natalie Piniuta. A huge shout-out to the Graham Elliot restaurant family and in particular John Slack, Georgia Vinzant, Angel and Ernesto Delgado, James Meek, Brian Runge, Joe Campagna, and Vincent Alterio. Thanks, guys, not only for keeping the ship afloat while I focused on the book, but for upgrading the ship and continuously steering her in the right direction.

To my editor, Leslie Meredith and her team at Atria books—with a special shout-out to Donna Loffredo—who shared my vision from day one and helped make this happen.

To my agent, Cait Hoyt, and everyone at CAA who worked so hard—sometimes into the wee hours!—to get this book off the ground. I also owe a big thank-you to my business manager, Zach Field; my talent agent, Lisa Shotland; and Michael Donkis, who does such a masterful job of public relations.

To Anthony Thalier, whose pictures capture the spirit and flavor of my food, and to my cowriter, Mary Goodbody, who held my feet to the fire even while holding my hand through this whole crazy cookbook-writing process. Without both of these amazing individuals, you'd be holding a couple of jotted-down notes with some drawings of food!

To everyone at Fox and on the set of *MasterChef* and *MasterChef Junior*. I especially want to thank Gordon Ramsay, who has believed in me since we first met nearly 20 years ago and who has had my back dozens of times. I also want to thank everyone at Endemol Shine North America, including Eden Gaha, Anna Moulaison Moore, Robin Ashbrook, Adeline Ramage Rooney, Brian Smith, Yasmin Shackleton, Drew Lewandowski, Joe Bastianich, and Christina Tosi.

There are others I can't forget, good friends who make life that much better: Dr. Vivek Prachand, who helped me get healthy; Dave Coligado, who trained me for my first marathon and continues to push me to new heights daily; Megan Doheny, who is such a close family friend she might as well be part of it; and Jason Budd, my bestie since high school (which is pretty cool considering how often I changed schools and addresses).

Big thanks to my mom, dad, and brothers for instilling in me an appreciation for travel, all cultures, and a thirst for knowledge.

And last but not least, I am grateful to the chefs who influenced and mentored me over the years. My journey would have been very different without these talented kitchen wizards: Matthias Merges, Giuseppe Tentori, Colby Garrelts, David LeFevre, Rick Tramonto, Dean Fearing, Stephen Pyles, Todd Jurich, David Lapinski, David Bull, and Michael Kramer. And to Charlie Trotter and Homaro Cantu, two inspiring artists and visionaries who are now cooking with the angels up above.

Index

About the Authors

GRAHAM ELLIOT is a critically acclaimed chef, restaurateur, and television personality who costars with Gordon Ramsay on Fox's hugely popular *MasterChef* and *MasterChef Junior*. He has traveled to all fifty states in search of the best food America has to offer, and in 2008, his eponymous Chicago restaurant became one of fifteen restaurants in the United States to hold two Michelin stars. He has been nominated for multiple James Beard awards as well. Graham, who used to play in a band and is a singer and guitarist in his own right, is the culinary director for Chicago's Lollapalooza, ranked as the third largest music festival in the country and one of the largest in the world. He lives in Chicago with his family.

MARY GOODBODY is an award-winning writer, cookbook editor, consultant, and recipe developer who has worked on more than fifty books with many well-known chefs, cooks, and food celebrities. She was a senior editor for the culinary website Cookstr.com and is the editor and content provider for Familytime.com. She lives in Fairfield, Connecticut.